THE

WALDORF-ASTORIA

COOKBOOK

Conrad N. Hilton (at left), Chairman of the Hilton Hotels Corporation and Hilton International, with Frank G. Wangeman, Senior Vice President and Director of the Hilton Hotels Corporation and Executive Vice President and General Manager of The Waldorf-Astoria.

THE

WALDORF-ASTORIA

COOKBOOK

Text by Ted James

Bramhall House · New York

CONTENTS

ACKNOWLEDGMENTS

Without the cooperation and enthusiasm of the staff and management of The Waldorf-Astoria this collection of recipes and social history would not have been possible. Special thanks are accorded to Frank G. Wangeman, Executive Vice-President and General Manager of The Waldorf-Astoria; Eugene R. Scanlan, Vice-President and Manager; Lola Preiss.

In addition, thanks to Ceil Dyer, the noted home economist who tested the recipes for the home kitchen, and John Marshall, whose superb color photos of the specialties of the hotel appear in the book.

PROLOGUE

The Romance of Food

BY definition, the romantic is anything that evokes something distant in time and place. And certainly food can be included in the list of the most evocative substances on earth.

The mere aroma of a superb boeuf bourguignon brings to mind the streets and alleys of Paris, the small café where you enjoyed your first dinner in the City of Light.

The taste of a peppery creole dish will take you back to New Orleans, the sultry evenings in the French Quarter.

A fine goulash will evoke Budapest, the romance of the Gypsies, the music of the soul. And a chicken Kiev, the days of Czarist Russia with all its pomp and splendor.

The bouquet of a fine wine will bring to mind the French countryside during the autumn harvest, with the orange sun casting a luminosity over the landscape, or an evening spent with dear friends in relaxation.

There is no question about it. The foods and wines of the earth are among the most romantic elements in existence.

Perhaps the greatest romance for us here at The Waldorf is the fact that we are feeding people from all over the world, ascertaining their likes, dislikes and their different tastes and doing our best to please their palates. The old expression, "The way to a man's heart is through his stomach," couldn't be more true. A man is definitely at his best when he has finished a satisfying meal. Perhaps the greatest problems in the history of world politics have been settled over the dinner table. And this goes for the greatest business deals as well, not to mention the affairs of the heart.

Here in New York City, we have access to all of the finest foods and wines on earth. The fruit and vegetables are fresh. They may come from the continental United States, Central or South America. Fresh scampi are flown from Spain, seafood from California. We can put our hands on things readily, whereas chefs in other cities cannot. We have the first pick, as most everything comes here first.

Primarily, what we try to do is to please the person we're cooking for. We want to please not only the Indian Prime Minister whose tastes are very esoteric, but the man from Iowa who knows and likes simple cuisine. It is as important to us to prepare the best corn in the best way possible for this man as it is to create a soufflé for General de Gaulle. The man knows what fresh corn is. A Tennessean knows the value of the finest smoked ham. We want to be sure that he gets the best, also.

And now just a few words of advice to you. Don't be afraid to change these recipes if you like. Add spices or a thickener or salt. Suit your taste and your family's. This is not a book of law or medicine which says you must not stray from the written path. If you wish to make changes, by all means do so.

Secondly, be adventurous. Try something you've never had before. That's what makes it fun. Try something you've never experienced, for there is nothing duller than eating the same thing all the time.

And finally, the most important thing in cooking is to buy only the very best ingredients. Purchase the best fruit, the best vegetables and the best meat. Buy with the same caution and care you'd use in selecting a new car or a new house. You'll pay a few pennies more, but it will be worth every penny. When you start out with the best, you end up with the best. All of the spices and sauces on earth will not make a poor piece of meat good.

Bon appetit,

EUGENE R. SCANLAN
Vice President and Manager

PART ONE

In the Beginning

THERE were several things one simply didn't do in 1893. The list of don'ts stretched formidably from one end of Fifth Avenue to the other. At the top of the list, however, underlined, circled and in italics, was don't number one: "We don't build a hotel, regardless of how sumptuous, how impressive, and how elegant, on Fifth Avenue in New York City." Fifth Avenue is where people live —in glorious brownstone mansions. One doesn't work on Fifth Avenue, one doesn't go out to dine on Fifth Avenue, one doesn't entertain outside the confines of the walls of one's Fifth Avenue mansion, and certainly one doesn't go to a hotel which is located on Fifth Avenue. Hotels are for travelers and out-of-towners. Everybody knows that.

Thus, when William Waldorf Astor announced that he was going to erect the largest and grandest hotel New York had ever seen at Fifth Avenue and 34th Street, there was talk of a monumental snub. There was talk of legal action. The Fifth Avenue denizens were in a snit. "Think of the neighborhood. It's the end of Fifth Avenue. First the buses and now this." Nevertheless, Astor, who had recently lost a Congressional election in this very same district and who had already prepared to get out of town to set up residence in the British Isles, tore down his house and erected the 13-story Waldorf Hotel on the corner of Fifth Avenue and 34th Street.

Whether the deliberate slap in the face of the group which had failed to send "Wealthy Willie" to Congress was due to a fit of pique or whether it was a simple matter of sound financial investment has never been ascertained. For whatever reason, sound it was, for the slap in the face of society turned out to be just a little tweak on the cheek, as society did come around and embrace the Waldorf Hotel as a new center for not only dining, but entertaining as well.

Witness the opening, March 13, 1893. It was damp, raw and wet. Mrs. William K. Vanderbilt had booked the brilliant young conductor Walter Damrosch and all the boys from the New York Symphony Orchestra for the evening. She had planned a quiet concert "at home," but decided to relinquish their services in favor of a benefit concert, to be held at the new hotel, for St. Mary's Free Hospital for Children, her favorite charity. Now, Damrosch could be counted on as a good draw. The sumptuous new hotel was an item of curiosity. Throw in Mrs. Vanderbilt and the waxworks assembled. From Chicago, NOT the butchers, BUT Mrs. Potter Palmer and Mrs. George Pullman in one of her private pullmans. And from Boston, deigning to make the trek, Lawrences, Amorys, Lowells, Peabodys and Dexters. From Philadelphia, Biddles, Lippincotts, Cadwaladers and Drexels. And, of course, from New York, Fishes, Hamiltons, Havermeyers, Jays, Lorillards, Morrises, Dodges and all those people.

The men selected as ushers at the concert "represent the flower of the Union, Knickerbocker and Calumet Clubs," to quote *The New York Times* of the day. At any rate, there was no ballroom fodder at this affair. It was strictly glitter, dazzle and glow from start to finish. And it put the Waldorf "in" with the jet set of the day.

Some 1,500 super society celebrities traipsed through the downpour to view the new Hotel Waldorf. One by one the guests disembarked from their carriages and swept into the palm-bedecked great drawing room, where the ladies of the committee received in their second-best gowns. The rainstorm had regaled a spirit of sense instead of splash. And they inspected the edifice from stem to stern. They saw the five-million-dollar hotel with 450 rooms and 350 baths. They saw eight private dining rooms all arranged to serve the côtelettes de ris de veau, oysters, terrapin, glace à l'orange and glace fantaisie. One of these was an exact reproduction of the dining room of the old Astor

Looking down Fifth Avenue to the old Waldorf-Astoria. The Empire State building now stands on the site of the famous hotel which was torn down in 1929.

mansion which had formerly stood on the spot. Much of the old Astor furniture and service was used. The famed Empire Room was done in the style of the grand salon in mad King Ludwig's palace in Munich.

Since it was the Lenten season, no dancing was permitted. However, this hardly kept the Four Hundred times four away. Many of the late arrivals found no seats available for Damrosch's concert. The papers elaborately covered the opening. A reporter for *The New York Sun* wrote, "Louis XIV could not have got the likes of the first suite of apartments set apart for the most distinguished guests of the hotel. There is a canopied bed upon a dais, such as a king's should be. Upon this couch shall repose the greatnesses, and, looking about them, see many thousands of dollars' worth of fineries. Think of the joy of being great!"

The New York Times informed the public as well as society that "the opening of a large hotel by society is a frequent occurrence in England and on the Continent, where the handsomest and most renowned establishments in the various European capitals have been opened by royalty itself with festivities of a brilliant character. It is novel in this country."

And further, to ascertain the extent of the impact of the Hotel Waldorf on the manners and mores of the era, an anonymous society woman's comment on the entire proceedings: "Few homes have chefs. I gave a small affair of eighteen covers at Mi Carême; the game was spoiled, undeniably spoiled and the strawberries were so hard and green it was like biting chestnuts to try to eat them. Such of us, by the way, who do not keep these treasures (private chefs) permanently in our service are welcoming the Waldorf with its famous Philadelphia caterer. It will be one additional high-class place, and will thus relieve the pressure on the two or three other places where all society wants to get service and it will besides stimulate these places to better work through a feeling of rivalry."

And so the Hotel Waldorf opened and changed the ways of the American society which had initially snubbed the entire project. The opening, however, was marred by a tragedy which caused comment

that the hotel was possessed with a curse. Two workmen had fallen to their death during the construction, and now, amid all the revelry in the main rooms of the palace, a young storeroom worker caught her skirt in an elevator. When the elevator operator tried to assist her, the elevator shot up and the poor girl plunged to her death down the elevator shaft. Jinxed or not, the Waldorf was in business.

The opening party, however, was a mere harbinger of the glitter and glamor to follow. The year was 1897. Mr. and Mrs. Bradley Martin had returned from a two-year stay on the Continent. Prior to that, Mrs. Martin's father had passed on and left her six million dollars, from an estate that was thought to be in the neighborhood of $200,000. Mrs. Martin, a bit of a diamond in the rough, was determined to crash into the Four Hundred. It was said that the lady had two separate ambitions which induced her to throw the extravaganza which took place the evening of February 10, 1897. First, to round off her social career in New York with the most superb entertainment the city had ever seen. Second, she wished to have her ball surpass the famed Vanderbilt ball of 1883.

In anticipation, *The New York Times* wrote a few days before:

Guests will arrive at eleven P.M. at the 33rd Street entrance of the Waldorf. They will proceed to the second floor, where 15 rooms including the Astor dining room will be used as dressing rooms. Hairdressers, costumers and modisters will here assist the guests in their final preparations. Mrs. Martin has selected English, French and German history from 1500 to 1900 as the period from which costumes are to be selected.

After final preparations, the guests will descend to the first floor, the small ballroom, and be met by Mrs. Martin on a raised dais under a canopy of old tapestries from her mansion. Lackeys will announce the names of the guests and the characters they impersonate.

The furniture for the party was entirely Louis XV, with the

corridors decorated to imitate woodland bowers. They were completely covered with greenery and lit by miniature incandescent lights. The musicians' balcony, with Victor Herbert in tow, was covered with pink roses. Beneath the balcony, the guests found green-covered flirtation nooks, sylvan dells overhung with clematis gathered by an army of poor people in Alabama. Quadrilles of Honor kicked off the spectacle at midnight. Supper for the 750 guests was served in the Empire dining rooms.

The press covered the ball extensively. So did the church—in tirades of flaying criticism from the pulpit. There was such strong reaction from certain segments of the public that a rudely constructed bomb arrived at the Bradley Martin home the evening before the ball. Mrs. Martin refused to comment but said, "The motto of our house is 'silence.' . . . You know, what wisdom teaches. . . . It pays to be wise."

Some 200 policemen supervised the arrival of the guests that evening. Four hundred persons had been employed in putting up the decorations. Residents of the neighborhood were barred access to their own homes during the arrival period. There wasn't a flower to be bought in the entire city. Flowers were brought in from Boston and Philadelphia.

A minor mishap which created an undue amount of amusement and comment was the matter of quadrille precedence. Mrs. Ogden Mills had insisted on precedence over Mrs. Bronson in dancing the quadrille. She implied she would not attend the ball unless she had her way. Mrs. Martin was in a bit of a predicament; however, the entire matter was settled by the late arrival of Mrs. Mills. Mrs. Bronson's quadrille was already over by the time the lady arrived.

As for the costumes, they were perhaps the most elaborate ever seen in New York City. Many of the men were more careful in historical detail and makeup than the women. A young artist from Boston named Cushing was in fact thought to have gone too far in his impersonation of an Italian falconer of the fifteenth century. His costume consisted of full tights and a short jacket with a little cap and long

The Bradley Ball at the Hotel Waldorf held February 10, 1897.

locks, while a large stuffed falcon perched on his left wrist. The costume left little to the imagination. "As far as the figure was concerned and although historically correct in every detail it was so decidedly pronounced that he caused a sensation wherever he moved," quipped the *Times*.

One Mr. Florence, a rather large man, arrived costumed as the Shah of Persia. The policemen, footmen and cabmen were all duly impressed because of the lavish display of jewels on his headgear. His purple cap, around which was a fringe of pearls, was well covered with diamonds, several large emeralds and a pearl pendant. One police sergeant commented to another, "Wait 'til he turns around again. That's all real stuff he's got on his head."

Columnists had a field day with comments. To quote one:

A young man with stooped shoulders in the guise of a 17th century courtier stood on the walk for a few minutes. There was a whisper among a number of cabmen and onlookers. "Look at them legs . . . he's a pretty brave man to trust himself on those things." The entire crowd began to snicker as the youth hastily took refuge in his carriage. The police attempted to move back and silence the crowd, but soon the knobby knees and skinny legs even made them chuckle.

And more comments on the men:

> Absence of high insteps was noted. Generally the dainty shoes showed long, slender feet. In the men, however, the arched instep that is often taken as the index of aristocracy was missing. Some of the insteps, in fact, were unusually low.

One man was arrested for passing back and forth under the awning which covered the arriving guests. He was discharged, however, by a magistrate who said that citizens should have the freedom to pass on the streets regardless of the Bradley Martin ball.

A description of the proceedings reveals the opulence:

> It was a curious composite of clothes. Cleopatra in converse with a frilled and jewelled courtier of the court of Francis I. Over in one corner was a motley group composed of belles of the Louis XV period, and a quaint Pocahontas and several gentlemen picked from the cavaliers of the First Empire and the days of the American Revolution. Another group, equally motley, was Catherine of Russia in deep-green velvet and ermine, and crowned with diamonds, chatting most amiably with a Venetian of the time of the Doges, while a dainty Priscilla smiled her sweetest in rich clinging gear on one of those gaudy butterflies that fluttered around the throne room of Louis the Grand.

The Bradley Martins were not modest people. An old authority on dancing quadrilles has it that, when royalty is not present, persons may receive as king and queen. Mrs. Bradley Martin received as queen.

John Jacob Astor, her partner, was king. During the quadrille, swords got tangled in gowns and laces and courtiers tripped over them to the delight of the spectators and the despair of the dancers. Mrs. Martin danced as Mary Queen of Scots in a costume of black and red with about $50,000 worth of jewels decorating the dress.

The famed Oscar of the Waldorf said, "Perhaps there had never been anything like it since the court at Versailles." At any rate, Mrs. Martin didn't achieve what she had set out to do. The *Times* said:

> The ball, as great as it was, didn't live up to expectations in the number of guests who were present. It must take a place behind the Vanderbilt fancy dress ball of 1883 and about equal to the Academy of Design ball of 1889.

The criticism continued for months, until finally the Bradley Martins picked up lock, stock and barrel and sailed to live in London.

The year before the big ball, 1896, all of those funny Chinese people came to town. And yes, they stayed at the old Waldorf. On August 29, Li Hung-chang, Viceroy of China, Prime Minister, Minister of Foreign Affairs, Senior Guardian of the Emperor, Earl of Suh Chi, and Commander of the Northern Army trundled into the hotel. *The New York Times* of the day called him "the greatest foreigner and most powerful ruler that has ever visited the United States."

The steamship *St. Louis* chugged into New York Harbor at around two in the afternoon that day. And, to receive her, a gala reception by warships and pleasure craft. J. P. Morgan's private steam yacht, the *Corsair,* was among the bunch, with Morgan himself standing on the deck to greet the dignitary. However, even more impressive was the steamship *Mohawk,* which the Viceroy's countrymen had chartered. It was crawling to the waterline with Chinese. Chinese flags covered the ship, and Chinese cacophony and jubilation took over from stem to stern as soon as the dignitaries' vessel was within sight. First, a barrage of small firecrackers was launched, followed by the igniting of

Li Hung-chang.

larger firecrackers and finally by the explosion of several large bombs. Simultaneously dozens of Chinese beat metal drums while the rest of them screamed at a pitch which could be heard in Jersey as well as in Havana. To add to this, a combo played Chinese music. In short, it was a blast. Those on board the *St. Louis* claimed that the Viceroy made not even the slightest notice of the noisy reception.

The official welcoming party consisted of General Thomas H. Ruger and W. W. Rockhill, who was then Assistant Secretary of State. The Viceroy, upon meeting Ruger and learning of his position, inquired as to whether or not he was rich and, subsequently, how old he was. Ruger was embarrassed, but it was soon explained that these were routine and polite questions in China.

The seventy-four-year-old Viceroy wore a yellow jacket, capelike in appearance and rather worn, and over this a dark blue brocaded coat which opened to reveal a pale blue lining. Beneath his jacket he wore a scarlet shirt, embellished with a floral motif. *The New York Times* reported:

> His manner, while entirely free from any suggestion of hauteur, was that of one so accustomed to homage that he received it without betraying that he demanded it, expected it, or was at all conscious of it. He made no effort to keep up conversation nor on the other hand did he impress others that they must do so.

After docking, he was carried to the dock in a red plush chair by four sailors. Immigration proceedings were waived. And then followed the parade from Lower Manhattan to the Waldorf. Half a million people lined the streets. The caravan wended its way up West Street, along Broadway and then on to Murray Hill. The reception became less and less enthusiastic as the Viceroy proceeded, owing to the changing nature of the neighborhoods. First, the longshoremen on West Street, then brokers and merchants on Broadway and finally tourists and club types on Murray Hill.

When he arrived at the Waldorf, a crowd received him with a roar of enthusiasm. George Boldt and the renowned Oscar, maître d'hôtel, greeted the dignitary at the door. Included in the party were secretaries, the Viceroy's sons, interpreters, a Scottish physician, six attachés, two copyists, a gentleman guard and 12 servants; also a dozen or more cooks, with the head chef, a tall, skinny man of undetermined age. The *Times* reported:

> He is apparently thoroughly impressed with the importance of his position. Of course he could not speak to the hotel attachés and he did not seem to have any desire to do so.

Oscar had ordered a meal prepared for the Viceroy. It was to include terrapin Philadelphia and côtelettes de volaille duchesse and to be concluded with a glace fantaisie. However, immediately upon their arrival, the staff of Chinese cooks and chefs were dispatched to the kitchen, where they prepared the meal for the Viceroy. He brought not only his cooks, but his own stoves and several dozen one-hundred-year-old eggs.

That evening a banquet was held at the Waldorf. Li entered smoking and didn't stop smoking through the entire dinner. He carried a small silver bowl to spit into and was supported by two men as he came into the ballroom. The ex-ministers to China were hosts and the papers said it was possibly the queerest banquet that had ever been given in New York. The food served was international except, of course, for that consumed by the Viceroy. That was Chinese. He sat at the table with a black satin cap on his head. In the center of his forehead was a setting of brilliant diamonds with an enameled stone in the middle. On his right pinky he wore a solitaire diamond. The *Times* described the proceedings:

> Earl Li and his countrymen enjoyed the feast. The knives and forks, however, did not fit their hands well. Some of them, when eating, leaned forward, resting their forearms on the table and attacking the food with the appetites of Tartars.
>
> Earl Li, however, did not eat the foreigners' food. He sipped at the broth, then discovered the spoon, picked it up awkwardly and put it on the plate. As it didn't look right there, he finally put it down on the table. He did not finish the broth. He contented himself with breaking off a piece of crust from a roll and kept it in his hand, now and then nibbling at it for want of something better. The fish he liked better and nearly ate all of it. (This was filets de kingfish à la Tourville.) This was his last attempt to eat American food. He let the veal and grouse pass untouched. Of wine he drank sparingly. Only once or twice in a toast, he placed the glass to his lips, but at his side stood brimming glasses of Bordeaux and Champagne.
>
> Finally a Chinese attendant entered bearing Earl Li's real dinner. It consisted of three dishes. There was boiled chicken, cut

up in small square pieces, a bowl of rice and a bowl of vegetable soup. By his plate the servant placed two ivory chopsticks. Earl Li removed his cap and began in good earnest the assault on the savory viands from Cathay. He handled the chopsticks with dexterity, picking up the dab of rice as nicely as could be done with a fork. He did not handle the little bits of meat quite so deftly.

A wooden toothpick six inches long was handed to him by an attendant at the end of the meal. The Chinese Minister contented himself with a little use of his long little-finger nail.

Following the dinner were the usual speeches and then the exit by the Chinese into the smoking parlor to rest for a while before retiring. The curious crowded around, with the comments becoming more and more audible. Finally when one of his lackies lit a pipe for his Majesty, a whisper buzzed around the room that the Viceroy was actually smoking opium. It was, however, merely ordinary tobacco in a waterpipe.

On the last evening of the Viceroy's visit, every lady visiting the Waldorf received a basket of roses as a gift from Li Hung-chang. However, the diplomat was not around to receive thanks. In the noted inscrutable manner of the East, he had packed bag and baggage and departed for the Orient.

Another notable personage to pass through the portals of the Waldorf in the early days was Prince Henry of Prussia, brother of the German Kaiser, who came to visit New York early in 1902. A large banquet was planned in his honor by the New Yorker Staats Zeitung. Upstairs from the Grand ballroom was a great room which was used as a serving pantry. In preparation for the banquet, several hundred bottles of champagne had been opened. The army of waiters and busboys were busy breezing in and out of the hallway in single file with trays of various courses. Somehow or other in the process, several of the waiters stopped just long enough to knock down a few swigs of champagne from the open bottles. The maître d'hôtel, who stood near the door of the ballroom, watched the procession of waiters entering

MAJOR-GEN BARON VON STEUBEN
PRESIDENT OF THE GERMAN SOCIETY OF THE CITY OF NEW YORK 1785-1795

118th Anniversary Banquet
of the
German Society
OF THE CITY OF NEW YORK
Saturday evening, March eighth
at the Waldorf-Astoria

Menu cover from the German Society dinner, March 8, 1902. The guest of honor
was Prince Henry of Prussia.

Prince Henry of Prussia, the brother of Kaiser Wilhelm, was the guest of honor at
one of the largest and most impressive banquets during his visit to the old Waldorf-
Astoria in 1902.

and leaving the pantry like a hawk. Suddenly, the procession halted—no waiters, no busboys.

Inside the kitchen, the waiters, predominantly French and German, had recommenced the Great War. The battle between the French and the Germans for the posssession of the champagne country and Rheims was in full swing. Evidently, one of the French waiters had passed a remark about the Kaiser and Prince Henry. One word had led to another and soon everybody was at each other's throats. Even the Italians had taken sides in the battle. The maître d'hôtel charged into the room, sized up the situation and called the house detectives to straighten out the mess. Order was eventually restored.

However, as the evening progressed, the wine steward noted that the champagne was disappearing at a rather phenomenal rate. Seems the corps of busboys were stashing it away in their trouser legs. An inspection was called. The busboys stood at attention as the steward passed down the line. Along about the middle of the line, one of the youths began to perspire. He gasped, and immediately a bottle smashed to the floor, with the wine splashing in all directions. As the inquisitor was about to grab the busboy, a second crash was heard down at one end of the line. Another bottle had slipped from its moorings and crashed to the floor. And then, still another. Before the inspection was finished, some ten bottles of the fine wine had met a similar end.

Prince Henry, rest assured, had his fill of fine food and wine and never got wind of the kitchen fracas.

The year was 1919, November 18 to be exact, just one week after the Armistice had been signed in Europe, when who should arrive on the scene but the handsome, dashing young heir to the British throne, Edward, Prince of Wales. Needless to say, invitations to various dinners and entertainment planned for him in conjunction with his visit were sought avidly by everyone who was anyone in New York.

And the first dinner given in his honor was held at the Waldorf. Little did the young Prince realize at that time that one day, as the Duke of Windsor, he and his Duchess would reside in the Waldorf

Towers, where they live to this very day when in New York. The
dinner on the evening of November 18 was given by Mr. and Mrs.
Pomeroy Davis on behalf of the former War Council and their asso-
ciates of the American Red Cross. *The New York Times* said:

> The dinner was one of the most notable functions staged in
> this city in recent years. The grand ballroom was more lavishly
> decorated than perhaps it ever had been before, being converted
> into a veritable spring bower through the liberal use of red roses,
> palms, contrasting shades of ferns and autumn leaves. . . . The
> men in formal black and white, the women resplendent in multi-
> colored evening gowns and sparkling jewels were representative of
> the best in the social, philanthropic, and business life of the
> community.

And further:

> Invitations had been strictly limited. . . . There was no
> overcrowding to spoil the picture. The top gallery was almost
> hidden behind greens, and was kept empty except for the orches-
> tra, while all the boxes on the first tier were occupied. Limited
> time was available for dinner as the Prince was off to the [Metro-
> politan] Opera, so the dinner was less elaborate than might have
> been expected.

The Prince entered the ballroom and took his seat at dinner.
Oscar of the Waldorf stood directly behind him. Oscar later recalled
that a large thronelike chair had been stationed at the table where the
Prince was to sit. Upon seeing it, the Prince demurred and commented,
"Oh, no, Oscar, it's too big." After the seating arrangements were
settled satisfactorily, he greeted the assembled guests briefly, but in a
very jolly manner.

And then the toasts. First, to President Wilson; then, to King
George V; and later, to the Prince himself, while the orchestra played

the proper national anthems. *The New York Times* mentions a stirring moment:

> General Pershing, who sat on the right of the guest of honor, declared in ringing tones that if ever again the principles of liberty, humanity and justice are put to the test, the men of America will again be found shoulder to shoulder with the men of Great Britain fighting in a common cause.

Following this, the Prince rose to his feet. He had changed the military dress he wore when he disembarked from the battle cruiser HMS *Renown* at her berth in the Hudson opposite 86th Street. He wore civilian evening dress with the wide blue ribbon of the Order of the Garter, the British Military Cross, the Croix de Guerre, the Order of Leopold and the Indian Durbar Medal, as well as the coronation medals of his father and his grandfather.

In reply to the speeches by the host, Mr. Davison, and Elihu Root, he praised the organization and spirit of the American troops, the readiness with which they adapted themselves to the terribly exacting conditions, the comradeship in arms of the Americans and the British "in the crisis of the war when our hope of victory seemed to hang by a thread."

Following the dinner, everyone hurried off to the opera. The scene there was rather more festive. The Prince took his seat in the Morgan box in the very center of the Diamond Horseshoe. A special concert had been arranged with selections from the third act of Saint-Saëns' *Samson and Delilah,* with Florence Easton, Caruso, Amato and Laurenti in the cast.

A society editor described the event. "Tiaras glinted and gleamed. . . . The startling hues of slowly moved ostrich feather fans . . . the splash of color from a sash of some foreign order." The Prince's box was decorated with laurel ropes, white chrysanthemums and bunches of American Beauty roses.

The orchestra played "God Save the King," and the *Times* described the Prince.

A rather tall young chap in full dress, the blue sash of the Order of the Garter across his chest, stepped into the box. The flaxen blondness of his hair was heightened by the flush of embarrassment in his cheeks. He stepped almost timorously into the fore of the box as Admiral Halsey, Viscount Grey and others followed into the enclosure.

"Three cheers for the Prince of Wales," shouted a plump, gray-haired man who sprang to his feet in the second row of the orchestra. And three good lusty cheers rang out with the Diamond Horseshoe putting as much if not more vigor into it as did the folks way up toward the top of the house.

The Prince nervously pulled at his cuffs. The audience laughed at his nervousness. He then tried smoothing his hair, then used a handkerchief. Following this, he was visibly more at ease.

Evidently he found it difficult to reach his box as hundreds of fashionable women and girls crowded around him. Several caught him by the arm "and he smiled on them as he was rushed along."

At intermission, he managed to find his way to Mr. Davison's box, where he inquired if he might smoke. Mr. Davison said that it was quite against the rules, but if he would like, they could make a trip down to one of the smoking rooms. The Prince agreed and arm in arm the two made their way down. Davison apparently smoked one of the Prince's cigarettes. And then, one young matron rather rocked him and caused him to laugh heartily when her comment reverberated around the room like the Annunciation in stereophonic sound: "Oh, isn't he cunning!"

On November 20 a dance was given on the roof garden of the Waldorf by the staff and members of the Motor Ambulance Corps for officers of the *Renown* and the *Constance,* and for the American warships *Delaware* and *Columbia.*

Chauncey M. Depew, a former Senator, then in his nineties, fondly recalled the visit of the Prince's grandfather 59 years before. He reminisced and mentioned that at West Point, "with some choice spirits among the cadets, the Prince had a night off." Prince Edward glibly commented later, "Well, I must say that grandfather did better than I have done. I haven't had a night off at West Point or anywhere else for that matter."

Another visitor from England arrived at the Waldorf in April of 1922. Lady Nancy Astor, an American woman of the Langhorne family of Virginia and the first woman ever to sit in the British House of Commons, was honored at a luncheon. Now, Lady Astor was, to say the least, a rather outspoken woman, and true to form, during her speech at the luncheon she gave the press and hence the American public a few things to chew their gums about.

She referred to her husband, whose family had founded the Waldorf, as Lord Astor, Member of the House of Lords, and as for her comments:

On New York: "I don't know any other place that has as good air as you have in New York nor any place where it's appreciated less. Here, most people have their windows closely shut and the steam turned on." Note to all members of Citizens for Clean Air, Inc.

On elegance: "Nothing is worse than expensive clothes for people who cannot afford them. I deplore the effort of the girl in moderate circumstances who tries to copy the clothing of wealthy women she sees. The wealthy women who dress that way would be helping the world more if they kept their fine clothes for the home and not for the street."

On Prohibition: "You'd better thank God you got rid of drink. If the rich want to drink, let them, they're not hurting anyone but themselves. What I'm thinking of is the poor man and his children who've never had a chance. Wines in France . . . many have too much to drink. And beer . . . only look what it did to the Germans. You know what two or three glasses of beer do to you . . . they make you drowsy."

On America and England: "If they are, as we say, the most advanced nations, then it's our absolute duty to help the others. America should take an interest in foreigners. Look how many she has here. Heavens, she has half of Europe right here in New York City."

On wives and mothers: "Wives come and go, but mothers stay on forever."

On the emancipation of women: "I supose all of you are desperately prejudiced against all women in politics. I don't blame you. I feel sorry for you."

On Lenin: "Mr. Lenin should know you can't drive human nature farther than it will go."

On men: "There's so much good in all men, but only good women can bring it out."

And finally a story she told about her return to her childhood home. The cook in the house, after having been shown a photograph of Lady Astor's English home, retorted: "I 'clare to goodness, Miss Nancy, you've just out-married yo'self."

The earful which Lady Astor delivered kept social circles in town twittering for weeks.

Some ten years later in the new hotel, in 1931 to be exact, during the Great Depression, Miss Ruth Vanderbilt Twombly, chairman of the executive committee of the Association for Improving the Condition of the Poor, pulled off the Peacock Ball as a social and financial success.

The entire ballroom suite was engaged and lavish entertainment was provided. Albertina Rasch, one of the outstanding members of the *Ziegfeld Follies*, staged a "White Peacock Ballet," in which the ladies of the chorus were all gussied up like white peacocks. There was also featured a Parisian café, an Argentine tavern, a Cuban cabaret, a Russian cabaret and a New York cabaret.

The New York Times described the decor as follows:

The smaller ballrooms and foyers were under the spell of a bizarre motif for the night. They represented a "Night Tour of Paris." The west foyer reproduced a taverne d'apache and was a baroque replica of La Cigale, the famous café of the Rue de Lappe in Paris. The typical effect of the bistro was enhanced by a bar for refreshments and authentic posters proclaiming the attractions of Parisian night life. French waitresses in apache garb were in attendance at many small tables in the room and occasional music was played by an apache orchestra under the direction of Miss Eleanor Kern, who sang several chansonettes of Montmartre. At about two o'clock an entertainment was presented in the Jade Room which had been transformed in keeping with the motif. Here, Nikita Balieff, maestro of the "Chauve-Souris," presented "Jar Pritza" as a Russian Gypsy night box. The soft green walls, classic columns and hangings of the room were blended into the decorative plan. Each pair of columns was flanked on either side by two stuffed peacocks, and huge candelabra stood on each side of the orchestra platform, behind which hung an illuminated Russian screen. Antique Russian brocade decorated the music stands of members of the orchestra, which played for the dancing and entertainment.

And, to add to the fun, a special nightclub was created in what was the Astor Gallery. For the ball it was renamed the Club Richman, after Harry Richman, who staged entertainment which included many of the stars from the *Follies*. Included on the roster were Helen Morgan, Ruth Etting, Mitzi Mayfair and Hal LeRoy. An additional charge was rendered for admission which helped the fund to improve the lot of the poor people.

And included in the evening's activities was the Rhuba Rhumba Cabaret in the Sert Room. And everyone had a nice time, except the poor people, who were all home trying to survive on oatmeal.

The Thirties, the Great Depression, and the New Waldorf-Astoria

ALONG with the thirties and the Great Depression came the brand-new Waldorf-Astoria. On October 1, 1931, the new hotel opened its doors to the public. There were more than 20,000 people assembled to pay tribute, including thousands who had lived in and loved the old Waldorf. This number of guests was almost twice as many as the number of invitations extended. Herbert Hoover hailed the building as an exhibition of courage and confidence on Opening Day in a brief radio address. The new Waldorf became a symbol of America's courage during the dark days of the Great Depression.

Oscar stood at the top of the wide stairs and greeted old friends. He was a committee of one. This was a day of triumph for the venerable old host of New York's world-famous hotel. The younger visitors, not yet imbued with the traditions of the Waldorf, made their way to the ballroom to hear a jazz band and to dance. Older friends arrived in vintage automobiles wearing the fashions of an earlier era. After the hour of school closing, hundreds of young people arrived. Most of the guests arrived early, while brokers and lawyers arrived in slight dishevelment after the day's work. An orchestra played military marches and American songs and rhythms which many recalled from the days of the old Waldorf.

And at dusk, Herbert Hoover addressed the nation from the Cabinet Room of the White House. The speech was piped into the public rooms and the ballroom, where the assembled heard these words:

Our hotels have become community institutions. They are the center points of civic hospitality. They are the meeting place of a thousand community and national activities. They have come to be conducted in far larger vision than mere profit earning. If we considered them solely from an economic point of view we should find them among the nine leaders of American Industry.

The opening of the new Waldorf-Astoria is an event in the advancement of hotels, even in New York City. It carries on a great tradition in national hospitality. It was one hundred and thirty-seven years ago that the first so-called great hotel opened in New York, the old City Hotel which was then heralded as an immense establishment, and which comprised seventy-three rooms.

It was visited from all parts of the country as one of the fine exhibits of our national growth. A long line of constantly improving hotels from that day to this has marked the measure of the nation's growth in power, in comfort and artistry.

The erection of this great structure at this time has been a contribution to the maintenance of employment and is an exhibition of courage and confidence to the whole nation. This occasion is really but the moving day of an old institution with all its traditions of hospitality and service into a new and better structure. I have faith that in another fifty years, the growth of America in wealth, science, and art will necessitate the institution's moving again to an even finer and more magnificent place and equipment.

In closing, Mr. Hoover congratulated the management on the consummation of its plan for the magnificent new home perpetuating the Waldorf-Astoria.

This was a coup for the powers behind the new hotel. Presidents had dedicated power projects and memorials, but not in the recollection of anyone at the time had a President of the United States dedicated a hotel.

Mr. Charles Hayden, a banker and backer of the hotel, was the

The new Waldorf-Astoria.

first to register, upstaging a gentleman from Chicago who had hurried to New York to garner that honor. Not to be outdone, however, the man left the hotel and officially became the first to depart.

As for the first dinner to be served in the new hotel, that went to the King and Queen of Siam. The Sphinx Club was the first to engage the hotel for a large dinner party, with the Henry Street Settlement House first to engage the roof garden. The dining-room space was booked for weeks in advance. However, one first yet remained for that opening week. The special railroad siding for private railroad cars beneath the superstructure of the building had yet to be booked.

And so, the new Waldorf opened amidst all of the financial chaos of the Great Depression. It was not for ten years or so, however, that the hotel finally moved out of the red and into the black.

One of the most fabled personalities ever to hit the Waldorf was the late Elsa Maxwell, who dropped anchor in the Towers back in the 1930s and lived there in queenly residence until she died. Her penchant for throwing memorable parties and gathering around her the great and near great of the world has become nothing less than legendary.

In 1939, the Waldorf published a book entitled *The Unofficial Palace of New York*, subtitled *A Tribute to the Waldorf-Astoria*, in which Miss Maxwell contributed a chapter about her party-throwing at the hotel.

After moving into Apartment C on the forty-first floor of the Towers, she begins her party reminiscences with:

> Then that dark Svengali specter, "Party Urge," raised its horrid head. "I wonder if it would be possible to give a party in the Waldorf," I thought dreamily to myself. "Oh, no," I argued, "there is no Olivier (of the Ritz Hotel in Paris) and no Charles (of Claridge's in London). Without one of that immortal duo I could never give a party. Besides, a party would be in danger of becoming lost in the labyrinth of this gigantic edifice.

I telephoned to what is known as the "Banquet Department" and told someone who answered the phone that I had to give a party at once, and who was I to see about it? Before I put down the phone, like a jack-in-the-box, or *"diable aux boiteux,"* up popped a tiny little man with sparkling dark eyes who murmured, as he bowed from the waist, that he was Captain Willy. I felt like saluting, and there began a relationship which will last, I fear, to the end of my days. For it is Captain Willy, the small, mysterious, sphinxlike maître d'hôtel, who guides my parties. I have to admit that in Captain Willy I have met my Waterloo, and the only reason for the continuing and ever-growing extravagance of my triannual routs, or costume balls, is the vain, mad endeavor to break down Captain Willy, to beleaguer and invade his calm and smiling "Yes, Miss Maxwell," which inevitably greets my wild and seemingly impossible demands.

Miss Maxwell continues:

When I suggested, casually, turning the Empire Room into a red and white stick of candy, expecting Captain Willy to object, or at least to murmur that it was quite impossible to do away with Empire chandeliers, mirrors, and decorations, the "Yes, Miss Maxwell" was almost too much to bear. But I gave the red and white party. It was a Burlesque Ball, a bit of striptease, Edgar Bergen, and nearly all the vaudeville acts that today make up the famous *Helzapoppin* at the Winter Garden. No one in the world could have suspected that under the red and white paper ceiling and walls of that room there really lurked the Empire Room.

In regard to that party, Jerome Zerbe, who was present, says, "It was the best party I have ever attended." A legitimate stripper had been hired to appear on the stage along with Reggie Gardiner, Elsa, the late Bert Lahr, and Bea Lillie. When the music started, the stripper, taking the entire production seriously, commenced to strip. Elsa and company

Elsa Maxwell.

were busily camping away when the great hostess suddenly realized that the attention was not focused on the act, but on the stripper. Upon turning around to view the professional entertainment, she blanched and had to interrupt the act for the sake of the sensitivities of the guests.

One of Elsa Maxwell's most memorable extravaganzas was her famous barnyard party. Her comments follow:

Then there was the time when I couldn't get the Starlight Roof for a party, as it had already been assigned to somebody else. I grew angry. I had already issued invitations for a ball on a certain date. The idea I had not yet found. "What room can I give my ball in?" I demanded in desperation. "There is the Jade Ballroom and the Basildon Room." I was led into the very modern, green, gold-pillared Jade Ballroom. You see, I love the Perroquet Suite (the most sympathetic room) for a small party, and the Starlight Roof for a large one. These two rooms give everything necessary to form the background and atmosphere for a successful party. . . . I turned on Willy, saying to myself, "Here is my chance. This will break him down. I'm going to hear 'no' fall from his lips at last, followed by the sweet word 'impossible.' " I said, "Captain Willy, in this Jade Ballroom, I am going to give a farmyard party, a barn dance. I'm going to have trees with real apples on them, even if the apples have to be pinned on. I'm going to cover those enormous chandeliers with hayricks. I'm going to have clotheslines stretched across the ceiling on which the family wash will be hung. I'm going to have a cow that milks champagne on one side and whiskey and soda on the other. I'm going to have a beer well. I'm going to have stalls with sheep, real cows, donkeys, geese, chickens and pigs and a hillbilly band"; and, as I stopped for breath, expecting to hear that word I had longed to hear for years, "Yes, Miss Maxwell," said Captain Willy. "Certainly."

To my surprise, I blurted out, "Impossible. How are you going to get live animals to the third floor of the Waldorf? What about the parquet floors?" "We can have felt shoes made for the animals," said Captain Willy firmly, and then I seized his hand and wrung it warmly. He was certainly a great colleague, though he broke me down.

Well, that barnyard party occurred—and made history on Park Avenue. Captain Willy produced from some traveling circus all the requisite animals. Leonard C. Hanna and Cole Porter found a champion hog caller, Tom Bevington, from Cleveland, and I procured a dozen great hogs who answered Tom's calls in the prescribed way at the right moment. They did clamber over a

Cole Porter and Elsa Maxwell.

few lovely ladies who, as beautiful milkmaids, were gossiping on a haystack, but after their screams of terror they stuck it out like grenadiers. Mrs. Henry G. Gray, one of my greatest friends, and Mrs. Guy Carey, another dauntless one, led in the square dances. Mr. Bert Lahr came with Bea Lillie and sang his famous woodman song, "Chop, Chop," and I have never, I believe, given a better party, or more intimate—in a ballroom.

But it is as much due to the imperturbable, undefeatable Captain Willy as to me that my parties at the Waldorf have taken place and will continue, I hope, to take place in the only hostelry that laughs.

Another one of Elsa Maxwell's memorable parties was one thrown in honor of Cole Porter's birthday. The party was held in the Starlight Roof Garden, with more than 400 in attendance for supper. All the guests arrived wearing fezzes, turbans and veils with their formal dress, in keeping with the title, "Turkish Ball."

The smashing opening of the show was the presentation of a tiny birthday cake by Miss Maxwell to Mr. Porter. The composer turned in scorn from the meager creation. Elsa then picked up a trumpet, played it and the curtains of the stage parted revealing a fifteen-foot-high birthday cake. Through the cake paraded personalities of the theater and motion pictures who presented their own renditions of Mr. Porter's songs. Among the stars were Tallulah Bankhead, Dorothy Sands, Gladys Swarthout, Mrs. Cornelius Vanderbilt Whitney, William Gaxton, Frances Langford, Bea Lillie, Ethel Merman, Victor Moore and Irene Bordoni. However, perhaps most memorable and most personal in the tribute to Porter was Elsa herself. In a crowning moment of her long career as an indefatigable hostess at the Waldorf, she sang "I Have a Shooting Box in Scotland," Mr. Porter's first hit, which he composed and wrote while an undergraduate at Yale.

With her passing several years ago, not only the Waldorf but New York and the world as well lost one of its most colorful and fun-loving personalities.

And, of Course,
Oscar of the Waldorf

M ANY personalities on the inside of the Waldorf have added to its colorful history. However, perhaps foremost of these is Oscar of the Waldorf.

During his life, he became one of the traditions of the hotel, known not only in New York and but around the world. Everyone knew who he was, and quite probably most of the great people on earth knew him personally.

Oscar Tschirky arrived in New York in 1883 from Switzerland, and first went to work as a busboy in the old Hoffman House on Madison Square. The Hoffman House was, in its day, the center of New York's more racy social life. And the owner himself, Edward S. Stokes, was rather a notorious figure around town. Born of a social family, he was the man who shot Jim Fisk after a scandal involving showgirl Josie Mansfield.

After serving four years at Sing Sing, Stokes was out on the town and ready to continue his escapades. He selected Oscar as his yacht steward. Several years later, Oscar moved on to Delmonico's, until one day he noted the beginning of the construction of the old Waldorf on Fifth Avenue. He approached the owners with some ten pages of endorsements signed by everyone from Lillian Russell to Diamond Jim Brady and was immediately signed on the line as head waiter. He remained that from December of 1892 until his retirement in 1943.

The late Oscar has been such an important part of the history of the Waldorf and its cuisine that it is perhaps better if his thoughts be

quoted directly from a chapter in *The Unofficial Palace of New York,*
published in 1939, two years after the Golden Anniversary dinner
presented by some 1,200 men and women in honor of Mr. and Mrs.
Oscar Tschirky:

"Almost all of us have souvenirs of one kind or another: They
may be photograph albums, autographed photographs, autographed
books, theater programs, scrapbooks of newspaper clippings, carefully
and honestly entered diaries—even if none of these, our precious memories.

"I have, I think, all of them. But what I cherish most is my
collection of menu cards—the menus of dinners served from the time
the first Waldorf opened its doors to the present day. For they provide
me with memories. They are reminiscent not only of sumptuous and
glorious dinners (with rare wines and many elaborate courses), but of
equally glorious friends and historical occasions.

"There are, in my collection, about two thousand such menus—
one of the largest collections of its kind, I've been told, in the world. To
me, each one tells a story. Indeed, I think of these menus as a history of
the past forty-five years, particularly as it concerns the Waldorf-Astoria,
the progress of New York society and the evolution of American cuisine.

"I am not thinking now of some of the more famous banquets
and suppers—such as the one that marked the opening of the hotel in
1893; or the dinner for Li Hung-chang, Viceroy of China; or the fare-
well dinner given by the Bradley Martins just before they left
America. My menus tell of many other dinners, long forgotten by me
until I began exploring them. Glancing through them, I was amazed
at the memories they brought back to my mind.

"Here, for instance, is a menu of a dinner for the Honorable
Clarence Lexow, on the night December 11, 1894. Lexow, as old-
timers will recall, was the Thomas Dewey of his day. His investigation
of graft and crime stirred New York. What particularly fascinates me
about this menu is its reminder of the numerous courses we used to

serve at public banquets. Today's average banquet is a 'snack' in comparison.

"Also there was the great variety of wines. We in America, perhaps because of the banal influence of the Prohibition era, have lost an appreciation of wine with meals—and that's a very great pity. Can you imagine an average banquet today during the course of which we are served Château Cerons; Amontillado Pasado; Saint-Estephe, 1888; Moet and Chandon, White Seal; Moet and Chandon, Brut Imperial; as well as an assortment of liqueurs? Yet paradoxically enough, those very wines were served during a dinner given by an organization called 'The Reform Club' on April 24, 1897. The speaker was a distinguished gentleman known as Grover Cleveland!

"Yes, they were lusty eaters—and drinkers—in those days. And this reminds me of a constant shift and change in our customs of dining and eating. What I mean is that I can separate my menus into five distinct periods, and each period will show, I think, a change in our tastes. For purposes of convenience and illustration, I've chosen five menus, each of which is representative of the nineties, the early nineteen hundreds, the war period, the Prohibition era, and the present, or New Deal, age.

"The dinner most representative of the lavish nineties, I think, was that given by Randolph Guggenheimer, then president of the Municipal Council, in February, 1899. It was served at a cost to the guests of $250 a plate. Nightingales sang in a grove of rose trees, grape arbors surrounded the banquet room, and a rare vintage of brandy, bottled before the French Revolution, was opened. Forty guests were present. Here is the menu:

MENU

Oyster Cocktail

* * *

Sherry

Lemardelais à la Princesse

Green Turtle, Bolivar

* * *

Rauenthaler Berg

Basket of Lobster

* * *

Colombine of Chicken, California Style

* * *

Champagne

Roast Mountain Sheep with Purée
of Chestnuts

Jelly   Brussels Sprouts, Sauté

New Asparagus with Cream Sauce

* * *

Fancy Sherbet

* * *

Diamond Back Terrapin

* * *

Burgundy

Ruddy Duck

Orange and Grapefruit Salad

* * *

Port Wine

Fresh Strawberries and Raspberries

Vanilla Mousse

Liqueurs   Bonbons   Fruits

Cigars and Cigarettes   Coffee

"Compare this with a menu for the nineteen hundreds. I select one for a dinner given by the Ohio Society of New York in honor of William Howard Taft, then Secretary of War, on the night of March 5, 1904:

MENU

Graves Supérieur   Cocktail aux Huitres

POTAGE

Consommé de Volaille, Printanière

Tortue Verte Claire

HORS D'OEUVRES

Radis Olives Celeri Amandes Salées

POISSON

Coquilles de Bass à la Virchow

Concombres Marines

ENTRÉE

Medoc Supérieur   Couronne de Ris de Veau avec
Champignons Frais

Champagne   PIÈCE DE RÉSISTANCE

Mignons de Filet de Boeuf à la
Cardinalice

Pommes de Terre Sautées en Quartiers

Petit Pois à la Française

Fond d'Artichauts Frais à la Dubarry

Sorbet de Fantaisie

GIVIER

Pluviers d'Herbes Rôtis

Gelée de Groseilles Salade Chiffonade

ENTREMETS DE DOUCEUR

Glaces à la Grenadine, Petits Fours, Fruits

Cigars   Café

"Another, on February 14, 1906, echoes a famous name. The guest of honor was the promising young president of Princeton University—Dr. Woodrow Wilson. A few nights later, a dinner was held in honor of the Right Honorable Earl Grey, then Governor General of Canada. On April 18, 1910, a dinner in honor of Britain's Field Marshal, Viscount Kitchener of Khartoum, whose tragic and mysterious disappearance during World War I is still a matter for conjecture.

"Then the war enveloped the American people, and from 1917 to 1919, I find the outstanding menus in my collection few and far between. Once in a while, of course, there was a great dinner such as that given on June 22, 1917, for Guglielmo Marconi, inventor of the wireless. But here is a dinner that provides us with a typical menu of the war years. It was given the night of January 12, 1918, in honor of the courageous Myron T. Herrick, America's ambassador to France, who determinedly stayed in Paris even when the French Government and all foreign ambassadors moved out for safety's sake. Here is the menu.

MENU

Graves Sauterne	Huitres de Haute Mer
	* * *
Louis Roederer Brown Label	Potage Fausse Tortue au Madère
	Celeri Radis Olives
	* * *
Charles Heidsieck Extra Dry	Medaillon de Kingfish à la Mornay
	Concombres à la Française
	* * *
Charles Heidsieck Brut '06	Ris de Veau Braise avec Champignons
	Petit Pois Sautés au Beurre
	* * *
	Sorbet Prunelle
	* * *
	Poitrine de Volaille, Sauce Diablée
	Coeurs de Laitue, à la Russe
	* * *
Pall Mall Cigarettes Cigars Carolina Perfecto	Glaces Fantaisie Gâteaux Assortis
	Café

"With the passing of the war, America settled down to begin an era of onrushing prosperity. But it was also the era of Prohibition. I glance into menus, from 1921 on: menus for dinners to honor such figures as Charles M. Schwab (on November 10, 1921); a rising young bandmaster, Paul Whiteman (August 14, 1923); to Presidents Harding, Coolidge and Hoover—and I find one thing strangely missing: a wine list. Drinking with meals had become a furtive practice everywhere. It was a pitiful blow to the art of public banqueting.

"Another significant change was evident in this era, as my menus show. The banquets became less sumptuous—more, shall I say, utilitarian? Certainly, the courses had been pared down. For instance, a dinner in February, 1924, for President Coolidge. (Note the "Apollinaris" and "White Rock" but no mention whatever of any wines or liquors.) Here is the menu:

MENU
Canapé of Anchovies
Cream of Celery with Toasties
Celery   Olives
Aiguillette of Striped Bass Joineville
Potatoes à la Hollandaise
Medaillon of Spring Lamb, Chasseur
Asparagus Tips au Gratin

* * *

Breast of Chicken à la Rosé
Waldorf Salad, Mayonnaise

* * *

Venetian Ice Cream
Assorted Cakes   Coffee
Apollinaris   White Rock

"The year 1938 was crowned in December with one of the most important dinners of all, that of the National Association of Manufacturers, when the main speaker was the Right Honorable Anthony Eden, Britain's former Foreign Minister, who made a speech which developed into a ringing defense of democracy.

"I would be hypocritical, however, if I did not climax this discussion of my menu collection with reference to a dinner given in honor of the golden wedding anniversary of—well, I might as well use the right names—Mr. and Mrs. Oscar Tschirky. It took place on the night of October 7, 1937, and it was the proudest moment of my life. Twelve hundred men and women gathered to honor us. Among so many others, there were Mayor La Guardia and Dr. Victor Nef, Consul General of Switzerland, the country of my birth. Messages were received from the President of the United States and his entire cabinet.

"It was sponsored by sixteen organizations and a distinguished Dinner Committee under the leadership of Crosby Gaige, Chairman, representing the Wine and Food Society.

"But, from a professional standpoint, that dinner seemed extremely significant to me. (Bear in mind that I had nothing to do with the preparation of the meal. For once Oscar was being waited upon!) But from my years of experience in composing menus for Waldorf banquets, I had found that certain dishes were outstandingly popular. This menu was a combination of such favorites. The wines were selected by the Banquet Committee and managed to harmonize perfectly with the dishes they accompanied.

"This dinner, so brilliantly planned, helped to revive the halcyon days, long past, when elaborate banquets were the rule rather than the exception. From that day I became convinced that the age of leisurely dining was inevitably returning. I still fervently hope so. Here is the menu:

MENU

Buffet Russe

London Club Amontillado Fino	Clear Green Turtle
Tío Pepe	* * *
Imperial Amontillado	Olives Pecans Celery
	* * *
Wurzburger Sylvaner Riesling 1935	Brook Trout, Gourmet Cucumbers, Sour Cream
	* * *

Château Latour 1925	Mignon of Beef, Béarnaise
	New Peas with Lettuce
	* * *
	Kirsch Sherbet
	* * *
Musigny, Comte de Vogue, 1930	Gray-legged Partridge
	Wild Rice Currant Jelly
	Waldorf Salad
	* * *
	Golden Anniversary Dessert
	Wedding Cake
	Fruit
Courvoisier, 50 years old	
Liqueurs	
Cigars, Cigarettes	Coffee

"History was made in the old Waldorf. I remember the very room in which the plans for the Panama Canal were first made, and Philippe Bunau-Varilla, the famous French engineer, to whom the building of the Panama Canal was the shining goal of his life. I saw Bunau-Varilla in the Palm Room dining with Mark Hanna, the most politically powerful man in the United States at that time, Bunau-Varilla arguing for the Panama Canal cause, Mark Hanna telling him that it was difficult to change popular opinion, then in favor of a Nicaraguan route. I remember the day that Bunau-Varilla convinced Mark Hanna that his plan was the better—the day the Panama Canal was assured.

"Presidents and princes came to the Waldorf. I remember the genial Taft and his preference for baked apples for dessert. William McKinley, even before he became President and the frequent times he came to dine at the Waldorf. Teddy Roosevelt, Wilson, Harding, Coolidge, all men with simple tastes in food.

"It was a great occasion, the visit of the King and Queen of the Belgians to America. I remember how painters worked day and night redecorating an entire floor in the hotel . . . the royal entourage's arrival, forty people in the party with 160 pieces of luggage for the King and Queen . . . maids, secretaries, ladies-in-waiting . . . private telephone installed, six cooks assigned to prepare meals for the party.

"I remember the dramatic day when the survivors of the *Titanic* disaster arrived at the Waldorf, brought here by the Carpathia, to greet their relatives.

"I remember Admiral Dewey, King Carol of Rumania, traveling incognito when he was Prince, Prince Poniatowsky, Lord and Lady Decies, Cardinal Mercier, Lloyd George, Marshal Foch, Ambassador Jusserand.

"And, the great Americans . . . Charles M. Schwab, whose friendship I have cherished through the years . . . Dr. Nicholas Murray Butler, gentleman and scholar . . . Andrew Carnegie and his wise eyes full of vision, Anthony Drexel, Senator Coleman du Pont, Gordon Fellowes, Commodore Carey, Robert Goelet, the Vanderbilts, William K. and William H., McKay Twombley, Alfred P. Sloan, Jr., Charles Hayden, Augustus Nuller, Lucius Boomer.

"Buffalo Bill, who registered at the Waldorf as 'W. F. Cody, Nebraska,' Nat C. Goodwin, Lillian Russell, who was glamorous long before that word was lightly used; Diamond Jim Brady, glittering and generous; John L. Sullivan; Charles Frohman.

"And in years not so long ago, Ethel Barrymore, regal and beautiful, reminding me of her uncle, John Drew, Sir Beerbohm Tree, and his stories of England's 'Old Vic,' the Broadway figures of the old days.

"I remember, too, when it was decided that the Waldorf that had once been 'up-town' was now 'down-town' . . . and the day it was decided to close its doors, on May 3, 1929. I remember that day that dozens of people who had spent their honeymoons at the Waldorf came rushing to New York to buy a chair or a lamp from their honeymoon suites. Then came the choosing of Park Avenue and 49th Street for the site of the new hotel and the months that followed when the new Waldorf-Astoria was rising floor on floor into the sky.

"I remember the flurry of the day, before the hotel was open, before it was completed when the King and Queen of Siam came to this country and Lucius Boomer gave a luncheon for them there. They were our first royal guests.

"There is the handshake of President Hoover I remember, at the new Waldorf-Astoria; the smile of President Franklin D. Roosevelt, the smile of Eleanor Roosevelt and her kindness and sincerity. A procession of new celebrities who have come to the new Waldorf: Princess Miguel de Braganza, Mrs. Robert Ogden Bacon, Mrs. Graham Fair Vanderbilt, Grace Moore, Mr. and Mrs. Gerard Swope, General and Mrs. Cornelius Vanderbilt, John Hay Whitney, Jesse Lasky, Walter Wanger, Adolph Zukor."

To a great extent Oscar and his staff are responsible for the standards of hospitality and elegance which have become the hallmark of the Waldorf-Astoria.

One institution of the Waldorf during the Oscar days were the Monday morning concerts. A regular feature of the hotel, they were started by Albert Morris Bagby, who was a pianist in his own right and a pupil of Liszt in Weimar. These concerts became an important part of New York's social life. In the book *The Unofficial Palace of New York, a Tribute to the Waldorf-Astoria,* Mr. Bagby writes of these concerts:

"More great music has been heard in the Waldorf-Astoria—both old and the new—than in any other hotel in the world. For nearly half a century almost every distinguished artist in America has appeared there, since the day that marked the turning point in my series of concerts, or Musical Mornings, more than forty-five years ago, when Mademoiselle Nellie Melba came to sing for my subscribers shortly after her spectacular operatic debut.

"The roster of Melba's successors, both vocal and instrumental, reads like a musical roll of honor, and there is scarcely a single important artist who has come to this country and failed to join the list.

Caruso, for instance, appeared at the Waldorf during eighteen winters; it was a memorable occasion every time he sang.

"I first met Mademoiselle Melba at dinner at Mrs. Paran Stevens' in New York. I had just moved the scene of my recitals to the Waldorf, and naturally wanted, more than anything else, to persuade her to sing at one of them. After dinner I told her how thrilled I had been by her performances in opera, and asked if I might call on her next day. She agreed, and when I mentioned my hope of engaging her, she said she would gladly appear. My announcement of this coming event was greeted with skepticism but on the day of the scheduled concert the ballroom was filled to capacity.

"Then came a harsh blow. Mademoiselle Melba developed a cold and could not possibly sing. She was a good and loyal friend, however. She came to the concert and sat in a box, and after I had introduced the substitute soloist to the audience I turned to her box and said, 'You will sing for us next Monday, won't you?' 'Indeed I will,' she answered enthusiastically. The following week she did sing, and as only she could. From that day on, the success of the Musical Mornings was assured. . . .

"When I first went to the Waldorf the concerts were held in what was called the Prince of Wales Suite, not because the Prince (Edward VII) had ever stayed there, but because the furniture was some he had used on a visit to this country in 1859. Prince or no prince, the rooms were a decided advantage over my old quarters, since they could accommodate one hundred and sixty visitors. But they also proved too small. I soon had to rent the ballroom, which, with a connecting anteroom, could seat 400. At the first concert there, every seat was taken, and an equally large crowd had to be turned away. In 1898 when the Astoria opened, I moved to its larger ballroom. Since then interest in the concerts has increased annually; now there are more than 1,500 faithful subscribers who fill the spacious ballroom of the new Waldorf-Astoria, where the Musical Mornings have been held ever since the hotel opened its door.

"When I planned the first recital in 1891, I intended calling it, for want of a better name, 'Matinée Musicale.' I was discussing this one day, with Miss Louise McAllister, the daughter of Ward McAllister, and she disapproved strongly of the choice. 'Not, "matinée musicale," ' she said. 'That isn't English. Why not "musical morning"?' I took her advice immediately. Incidentally, Miss McAllister once told me an interesting story about her father which, as far as I know, has never been accurately recorded. It was about the origin of the title, The Four Hundred, which he is credited with having given New York society. This is how it came about:

"Late one afternoon a reporter called to see Mr. McAllister and to ask him if it was true that the city was going to buy a pier on the North River, I think it was Pier No. 2, belonging to Mrs. McAllister. As he was leaving, the reporter said, 'Oh by the way, Mr. McAllister, how many people do you expect at the next Patriarchs' Ball?' 'Well,' said Mr. McAllister, 'I suppose about as many as the ballroom at Delmonico's will hold' (the balls were later held at the Waldorf, of course). The reporter then asked how many that would be, and Mr. McAllister called through an open door to the library, where his wife and daughter were sitting, and asked them. 'About four hundred,' Mrs. McAllister called back. 'Thank you,' said the reporter, and left. The next morning, I remember reading that Ward McAllister has said there were only four hundred people in society in New York. And all because a reporter wanted to know if Mrs. McAllister was going to sell a pier to the city!"

Four hundred, perhaps. However, thousands of New Yorkers enjoyed the music of such artists as Kirsten Flagstad, Lotte Lehmann, Susanne Fisher, Irene Jessner, Giovanni Martinelli, Mario Chamlee, Richard Bonelli, Emanuel List, Ezio Pinza, Lillian Nordica, Emma Eames, Emma Calvé, Edouard de Reszke, Victor Maurel and Pol Plancon. And millions more ultimately enjoyed the fruits of Mr. Bagby's Musical Monday Mornings held at the Waldorf.

And to the Present

D URING and following World War II, the Waldorf-Astoria continued in its position as the grandest and most glamorous hotel
in New York City.

During the 1940s a group of dignitaries from India arrived at the
Waldorf and brought their own chefs with them. Indian chefs are very
polite people; however, when they do not speak English at all, problems can arise. And they did, in the kitchen of the Waldorf-Astoria.
After their introductions to the staff, the Indian chefs proceeded to try
to communicate exactly what they needed for the preparation of their
dinner. Their primary concern was to find a pot or casserole large
enough to contain their creation. That problem was shortly solved. The
biggest casserole dish in the entire world was lowered from a top shelf
and placed on the stove.

From there, the matter of ingredients was communicated by the
drawing of pictures. Rice, beef, lamb, chicken, fish and orange rind and
mangoes were all located and placed at the disposal of the visiting
cooks.

Now, it is a tradition in the Waldorf that hot food be served good
and hot and that cold food be served good and cold. As the cooking
commenced, the chef sampled the cuisine of the Indians and found it
altogether delicious and delicate in taste. After the simmering stage, the
Indians removed the casserole from the flame. The chef's concern
became evident as he feared for the cooling of the dish. Therein
followed an amusing series of attempts on the part of the Waldorf staff

to place the immense dish back on the flame, and the subsequent attempts on the part of the Indians to remove it. Shortly, the visitors raised the dish to a table and rolled it up to the forty-second floor. Chef Scanlan was still rather deeply concerned about a chilly dinner.

When the dish reached the room of the visiting Indians, the Waldorf staff found the entire dining room cleared of furniture. In the center was placed a beautiful Oriental rug. The gargantuan casserole was placed in the middle of the rug, and the diners sat down around the pot, folded their legs, and commenced to eat the meal with their hands. Now the chef understood why the food could not be served hot.

Another story involving the kitchen occurred shortly after the war was over. It used to be that the Board of Health in the City of New York permitted restaurants to maintain pets in the kitchen. And the Waldorf kitchen was no exception. There was a cat which lived in the kitchen of the Waldorf. This, however, was no ordinary cat. In fact, he was rather extraordinary. Nobody seemed to know where he came from, when he had arrived. He had always just been there. His name was Mr. Boomer, named after Lucius Boomer, then president of the hotel. He received this name because he had such dignity about him, much the same as the human version of the name.

Mr. Boomer, it is said, ate nothing but crabmeat. He had always eaten nothing but crabmeat. And he slept on the steward's desk in the Outgoing box—perhaps indicative of the fact that he considered himself quite independent and given a whim might just split the scene forever. However, he didn't. He stayed and stayed for years. And, he grew bigger and bigger until he tipped the scales at twenty pounds. Everyone knows that twenty pounds of cat is a lot of cat, and definitely not a creature to be taken lightly. Mr. Boomer, with all of his dignity, was not one for affection. Anyone who dared to try to pet him would receive a nasty little bite on the calf.

When he would spend time on a crate of oysters or a box of fruit, the kitchen would have to do without that particular food for the duration of Mr. Boomer's nap. To try to dislodge him from the spot would be taking one's life in one's hands. Nobody ever dared!

His forays into the outer world consisted only of trips in the elevator. And amazingly so, he seemed to know exactly where he was headed. He would only emerge on either the eighteenth floor, where some of the storerooms were, or on the second floor, where the kitchen was. There is not one record of his ever having emerged on any of the other floors in the hotel.

However, there is another story about Mr. Boomer. One morning when Chef Scanlan was emerging from the subway at Lexington Avenue and 51st Street, he noted a great deal of hornblowing and apparently a traffic jam. He walked to the corner, and there sitting smack in the middle of the intersection was Mr. Boomer. And he appeared as though he were determined to stay put. A policeman tried to move him, but of course was confronted with unsheathed nails and a rather nasty sneer. Eventually Mr. Boomer did pick up and go back to the Waldorf kitchens, but not before creating minor havoc in the midtown area.

When the Health Board decreed "no animals in the kitchens," the staff tried to get rid of Mr. Boomer, but to no avail. He went on living there for several years after the law had been passed. Then one day, he took heed of the Outgoing box, walked out of the Waldorf and was never seen or heard from again.

And still another four-footed denizen of the kitchens of the Waldorf ultimately became a legend. A lot of people keep turtles as pets. They're relatively easy to care for, never force their affection on you. However, on occasion they tend to wander from their provided home, almost inevitably ending up behind the refrigerator. And, at the Waldorf, there is on record a tale of a misplaced terrapin.

Terrapin soup has always been a great specialty of the kitchens of the Waldorf. And several years ago, a very special party was held at which the soup course was to be made of these rather toothsome creatures. The terrapin had been ordered, forty in all, and the chef commenced to count them. Terrapin are rather expensive so it is always a good idea to count them to be sure that you have received the correct number. In addition, the ingredients must be very exact, as not enough terrapin in the soup will tend to create a watered-down version of the delicacy. The chef discovered that there were only 39 of the reptiles in the shipment. A search immediately began. There were thoughts that perhaps one of the kitchen help had availed himself of the creature.

The terrapin was nowhere to be found. "On with the soup!" bellowed the aggravated chef. And so the soup was created. Now it is the custom at such dinners to have a tasting before serving the various dishes. The chef took his soup spoon to the kettle, tasted the soup, tasted it again, and just as he uttered the words, "It tastes weak," the vanished terrapin came trundling across the kitchen floor. He had been hiding under one of the refrigerators.

However, the story does not end here. Nobody wanted to cook the terrapin. He had won a place in the hearts of all in the kitchen. He stayed around for several weeks as a mascot, and then one day disappeared again. This time, however, forever. Could be that to this day somewhere in the maze of the kitchens of the Waldorf, the little terrapin still sits hiding under a stove or icebox.

And there are times when the best intentions of the chefs are shattered by forces beyond their control. During the late forties, General Charles de Gaulle arrived at the Waldorf-Astoria. The kitchen staff at that time was predominantly French, and for that reason a monumental effort was considered to be absolutely essential to assure that the food served to Monsieur le Général be absolutely perfect. All of the chefs were in a tizzy of excitement in anticipation. But quite possibly the grandest gesture of chauvinism was to be rendered by the pastry chef. Soufflés had always been his spécialité, and he decided to prepare for the General the most sumptuous and exquisite soufflé of his entire career.

The various members of the French community and of the American committee assembled in the ballroom for the dinner. Everything was planned to the most minute detail. The pastry chef, down in the pastry kitchen, had arranged for a closed telephone to be connected by direct wire from the ballroom. This, so that he would know at exactly which instant to pop his soufflé to end all soufflés into the oven. The salad had been served, and word went down to the chef from the headwaiter that the soufflé serving could be counted on at a certain time.

Shortly after the chef had placed his masterpiece into the oven, a rather well-meaning but unfortunately long-winded gentleman rose to deliver a speech honoring the General. Word did not reach the kitchen, as the headwaiter would not have dreamed that the man would speak on and on. The chef drew the soufflé from the oven, gleamed with satisfaction, and ordered the masterpiece to be delivered to the serving table in the ballroom. Into the elevator went both soufflé and chef.

Upon his arrival at the serving station, the chef found to his dismay that the above-mentioned gentleman was still rambling on and on about the glories of France and the accomplishments of the General. The soufflé sagged slightly in the middle. The chef grew apprehensive. The gentleman droned on and on and on.

Since the headwaiters were not French, they failed to realize that all good Frenchmen know that a soufflé must be served immediately after taking it out of the oven. To interrupt the speech with the clatter of serving would be out of order.

The chef became more and more distraught, as the monumental soufflé created especially for the General finally sank with a thud to the bottom of the dish. He took off his apron and, expressing his dismay and outrage, threw it to the floor.

A major gesture of emotion, granted; however, there is noted in the annals of soufflé history an incident which occurred in France during the last century. A similar delay of the serving and a similar fallen soufflé caused one pastry chef dramatically to grasp a carving knife and plunge it into his belly. He died.

Several years later, in 1952, the first of a series of extravaganzas to be held in the Waldorf-Astoria took place. It was the April in Paris Ball, which to this day is still one of the most fashionable social events of the New York season. The first bash cost some 1,200 people $25 and $35 a ticket. The price has risen rather substantially. However, many people consider not only the charity donation as being worthwhile, but also the fact that bundles of gifts are distributed to each donor which generally are in retail value worth almost as much as the donation. At the first ball, the ladies each received some six bottles of French perfume while the gentlemen received a silk ascot. Since then the bundles have grown, with perfumes, champagne, neckties, records, art books, cookies, jewelry and colognes, probably valued at around $100, going to each ticket holder.

At the first April in Paris Ball, the main ballroom was recreated into a great pleasure palace with an immense chandelier made of French lace hanging from the ceiling. Yards and yards of blue silk hung as a canopy from above and in the center of the room stood a creation made of mimosa which Air France had flown over from France especially for the occasion.

During the orgiastic dinner, chefs would step forward on the stage and announce to the assembled: "Mesdames et messieurs, I have the honor of presenting the pâté de foie gras de Strasbourg" or whatever the course happened to be. While this course was being served, four costumed waiters proceeded through the room carrying a display of a model of a white goose and an Alpine mountain of chopped liver.

In the meantime everybody sat and waited for the guests of honor, including those who were to participate in the spectacle planned. At 11:30, Queen Juliana of the Netherlands and her consort, Bernhard, made their entrance, kicking off the pageant.

And what a pageant! It was entitled "Love Through the Ages," and to start it off two ladies who played the lute sang medieval songs as Jarmila Novotna, the opera singer, entered as Eleanor of Aquitaine. Madame Claude Arpels of Van Cleef and Arpels impersonated Isabel of Flanders, Virginia Ryan was Ermengarde of Narbonne, and a barrelful of tumblers and acrobats from the Ringling Brothers, Barnum and Bailey Circus bounced around along with a dancing bear. When the bear had finished his act, Michael Fokine brought on a troupe from the Ballet Theater which he had directed and staged especially for the evening.

This, however, was only the beginning. For the second scene in the pageant, Henry of the Waldorf impersonated John Lodern, Mrs. Robert Kintner was Catherine of Aragon, Mrs. Thomas Phipps was Mary Tudor, the late Dorothy Kilgallen was Françoise de Foix, Phillip Van Rensselaer was the Duke of Norfolk. After the group had assembled, the lights were dimmed and a band of 36 Scottish dancers and 12 bagpipers marched into the ballroom and performed the Highland Fling by torchlight.

To add to the whoopee, Gilbert Miller, the theatrical producer, rode in on horseback as the Ambassador of China. He was followed by several elephants which had been coaxed into the ballroom on their knees, and finally by not only Elsa Maxwell but Beatrice Lillie as well impersonating Indian Ambassadors. The orchestra played from Rodgers and Hammerstein's *The King and I* as a little man carrying a broom finalized the procession.

This, however, was still not enough. The third act depicted the French Court under Louis XIV. Pierre Balmain played Louis and a group from the Comédie Française performed from Molière.

Following this, there was a fashion show represented by Christian Dior, Jacques Fath, Balmain and Givenchy. By the time dawn arrived some $20,000 had been raised for charity and, needless to say, New York had seen a production rarely equaled in the annals of the city's social history.

In addition to New York's most fashionable charity galas, the Waldorf is often host to the crowned heads of the world. On October 21, 1957, Queen Elizabeth II was due to arrive in the United States. She and the Duke of Edinburgh were flying into New York and naturally would reside in New York's Unofficial Palace, the Waldorf-Astoria. And it was presumed they would be staying in Suite 35A of the Waldorf Towers, the Presidential Suite, perhaps the finest accommodations available in the entire country for visiting royalty and heads of state. The suite, at $2,000 a week, is complete with four bedrooms, all with baths, drawing room, dining room, foyer and serving pantry. However, a major crisis was in the works, one that could perhaps put several noses out of joint.

There is an unwritten rule about Suite 35A. Heads of state always take precedence over temporary occupants. Among the rich, staying in this suite is a "must" as it is with leaders of society. Therefore, the tradition of vacating the premises gracefully is often *comme il faut*. There have been many occasions when Americans have bowed to rank. An American businessman happily vacated for General de Gaulle as did another to President Nkrumah of Ghana. When Mr. Khrushchev visited here with his family, the suite was made available.

So the management found itself in a rather difficult situation the morning of the arrival of the Queen and Prince Philip, because in residence in Suite 35A was Prince Faisal of Saudi Arabia. With great tact, they approached the Prince with news of the Queen's arrival and informed him as well of the tradition of vacating the premises. The Prince would have none of it. He explained that he was sorry, but he was ill and would certainly not move—and nothing which the management could say could convince him otherwise.

There is, however, another suite in the hotel just seven floors below the Presidential Suite which also has the tradition of vacating. That is Suite 28A, where the Duke and Duchess of Windsor stay when they're in town. And while the time for the arrival of the Queen and Philip grew closer and closer, the Waldorf staff shifted into high gear and gussied up 28A. By the time the royal party arrived, all was in order and the Queen and the Duke moved into the suite usually occupied by the Duke and Duchess. Nobody was the wiser, everything went like clockwork and an incident of international embarrassment was avoided.

Meanwhile, for days before, the Waldorf kitchen was full of the excitement which precedes a very important dinner. Preparations were being made for the banquet which was being jointly sponsored by The

Pilgrims of the United States and the English-Speaking Union, two societies devoted to furthering Anglo-American unity.

And not only the kitchen, but the entire staff of the hotel busied itself with the arrangements. At twelve noon on that day, the results of the organization were brought to fruition. The Queen first entered the Waldorf at the Towers entrance on the 50th Street side. The floor had been newly tiled and was covered with the famous red carpet reserved for heads of state. Conrad N. Hilton himself and other executives of the Hilton organization were on hand to greet the royal party.

The Queen and Prince Philip and their entourage—two ladies-in-waiting, the Queen's dresser, the Duke's valet, a page and a footman —stepped into the elevator and rose to the twenty-eighth floor, where they moved into the Duke and Duchess of Windsor's suite. The elevators had all been carefully checked by engineers from the Otis Company before the arrival. The special elevator used by the royal party had been reserved for them exclusively until after their departure.

As for security, there were included officials from Scotland Yard, patrolmen and hotel police provided by the hotel as well as city police, plainclothesmen and F.B.I. agents. This entire procedure was carefully organized in advance so that conflicts and security gaps could be avoided.

Suite 28A had been carefully arranged for comfort. The large off-white dining room with its coral-rose velvet-upholstered antique white French chairs had been further implemented with an inconspicuous bar in the corner. A large can of iced fresh beluga caviar with appropriate garni was placed on a table. In addition, the hotel provided their renowned hot hors d'oeuvres.

An hour later, after dressing, relaxing and signing the Waldorf's special guest register reserved for the use of heads of state, the Queen arrived in the Grand Ballroom for the luncheon which then Mayor Robert Wagner gave for her.

The Grand Ballroom, scene also of the dinner that evening, along with six smaller dining rooms, had been painted for the occasion. Fifty chandeliers glistened from the ceiling. Flags had been specially cleaned

A LUNCHEON IN HONOUR OF

Her Majesty Queen Elizabeth II

AND

His Royal Highness The Prince Philip,
Duke of Edinburgh

GIVEN BY

The Honorable Robert F. Wagner

MAYOR OF THE CITY OF NEW YORK

OCTOBER 21, 1957
WALDORF-ASTORIA

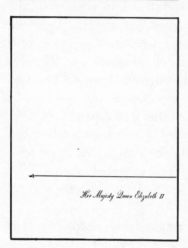

Her Majesty Queen Elizabeth II

His Royal Highness The Prince Philip,
Duke of Edinburgh

Program and menu from luncheon given in honor of

Queen Elizabeth II and Prince Philip, October 21, 1957.

and pressed. The help wore new uniforms and the staff of 500 food and wine waiters, 50 captains, 25 bartenders, 100 cooks and assistants, 100 stewards and dishwashers, along with ushers, security officers, elevator operators, cloakroom and washroom attendants, all performed their scheduled duties.

Then through the public address system:

"Ladies and Gentlemen: Her Majesty Queen Elizabeth II of England accompanied by the Chief Executive of the City of New York."

Three thousand guests rose to their feet. The orchestra played Sir Edward Elgar's "Pomp and Circumstance" and the Queen entered. She wore a printed taffeta afternoon dress with a small turban to match. The Mayor and Prince Philip were behind. They proceeded to the dais and the orchestra played "God Save the Queen" followed by "The Star-Spangled Banner."

The luncheon proceeded. Three courses only, at the bidding of the Queen. The menu is as follows:

MENU

Lobster Bisque Waldorf with Brandy

Johannesburg   Riesling,
   Almaden

Squab Chicken Manhattan with Wild Rice
Tiny Green Peas

*   *   *

Beaulieu Vineyard
George de Latour
Cabernet 1948

Delices of Raspberries
à la Royale

The Wines of the Country   Coffee

Included on the dais were such distinguished personages as Henry Cabot Lodge, Jr., Norman Robertson, Mohammed Ali, Gaganvihari L. Mehta, Sir Percy Spender, Selwyn Lloyd, W. Averell Harriman,

Herbert Hoover, Robert F. Wagner, Richard C. Patterson, Jr., Sir
Leslie Munor, Sir Harold Caccia, Dr. Ismail Rahman, Bernard Ba-
ruch, Abraham Ribicoff, Jacob K. Javits, Mrs. Franklin D. Roosevelt,
Dag Hammerskjold, Wiley T. Buchanan, Jr., John Hay Whitney,
Thomas J. Watson, Jr., Herbert H. Lehman, General Lucius D. Clay,
Henry Luce and Arthur Houghton.

By three o'clock the luncheon had terminated, and the Waldorf
proceeded to arrange for the dinner to be held that evening. The menu
follows:

MENU
South Carolina Green Turtle Soup

Chassagne   Montrachet   Long Island Striped Bass with
Morgoet 1955   Champagne Sauce and Golden Fleurons

* * *

Château Lascombes 1953   Filet of Beef with Truffle Sauce
Nest of Beignet Potatoes
New String Beans Amandine

* * *

Besserat de Bellefon 1949   Waldorf Savarin au Rhum
with California Nectarines
and Oregon Cherries
Golden Sabayon Sauce
Haitian Coffee

Preparations for the dinner had started several weeks before, initi-
ated by the arrival of a herd of ten turtles, each weighing 150 pounds.
A total of 4,500 pounds of filet of beef, 4,500 pounds of striped bass,
1,200 pounds of potatoes and 1,000 pounds of string beans were
ordered and prepared for the 4,000 assembled guests.

After a small private reception, the Queen, Prince Philip and the
royal party visited each of the dining rooms to greet the guests personally. Seven pipers of the Black Watch (Royal Highland Regiment) of
Canada preceded them. After the tour of the separate dining rooms, the

pipers escorted the Queen and party to the dais of the main ballroom. She wore a gown of multicolored lace with paillettes in iridescent shades of pink, blue and green, and tinted simulated jewels. Her tiara, necklace and earrings were of sapphires and diamonds.

The formal program commenced with remarks by former Ambassador Douglas, a congratulatory telegram from Sir Winston Churchill, introduction of Her Majesty by Hugh Bullock and then a speech by the Queen.

At exactly 11:10 P.M. Queen Elizabeth II departed from the hotel. And Suite 28A? Within an hour it was again filled with a distinguishd visitor—President Dwight D. Eisenhower.

Many stories involving royalty, titles and heads of state have added to the legend of the Waldorf. Several years ago Ibn Saud arrived with a herd of goats so that he could have fresh goat's milk during his stay. He also insisted that all beds be removed from his suite except his. The servants were to sleep on the floor.

And one day an Italian Countess checked in. The hotel was completely booked. However, one guest relinquished her room for the Countess. About two or three in the afternoon she moved in along with a pet alligator. And then she called the management to make a very strange request. She wished to have steps built into the side of the bathtub so that the alligator could walk up and down. The management obliged and sent a staff of carpenters to do the job. Shortly, a gentleman caller arrived, and as a gag kissed the alligator on the head. The alligator retorted with a quick snap and doctors had to be called to give the man a tetanus shot.

When John Glenn arrived in town a reception and luncheon was held in the ballroom. About 1,500 guests had been invited. The city extended the invitations by telegram, and the telegram itself was the ticket of admission. Luncheon was set for the 1,500 invited; however, some 2,000 arrived. The management shortly learned that many of the invitees had duplicated the telegrams and sent them to their friends.

At one time Prime Minister Menzies of Australia, the Prime

Minister of New Zealand, and Harold MacMillan, Prime Minister of England, were all waiting for an elevator. The Down button had been pushed for one of the ministers and the Up button for another. When the elevator arrived, the operator said, "Your elevator, Mr. Prime Minister." The three gentlemen stood there confused until Prime Minister Menzie commented, "There are so many damned Prime Ministers here, we don't know which one you're referring to."

Another time, Harry S. Truman was feted at a birthday party. When asked if he wanted orange juice, he retorted, "Get me bourbon and water."

And Prince Faisal once ordered toy trains to be placed on his table so that he could operate them during dinner.

Several years after Queen Elizabeth's visit, former Soviet Premier Khrushchev visited the United States and the United Nations, and he also stayed at the Waldorf-Astoria. If you recall, that was 1959, the year that everyone was in town. The State Department and the New York City Police were in a tizzy. Security had to be preserved at all costs. Imagine the consequences if one of the luminaries had been put to rest. Perhaps there have never been so many members of New York's finest on the streets. And not only the police, but spectators and demonstrators at every turn.

A reception had been planned for Premier Khrushchev; however, no specific time had been set. Twenty minutes before his arrival, the officials of the Waldorf were informed. Immediately, police barricades were set up in the lobby, a platoon of officers guarded the entrance, and Khrushchev was whisked through the crowds and into the hotel without an incident. This, incidentally, was the only time that the hammer and sickle has flown over Park Avenue in New York.

A luncheon had been planned by the city for Khrushchev. The American Dental Association had long before rented the Grand Ballroom for their convention. Upon being asked to move, they refused. Vice-President Richard Nixon opened their meeting with a congratulatory speech and followed it with the comment, "The Russians may have been the first to go into orbit. However, I am pleased to see that the dentists had the Waldorf for their meeting."

Khrushchev brought his own chef with him. But not because he was wary of the Waldorf's cuisine. He wished to have his chef observe how the Waldorf chefs do it. The Premier's chef was given the courtesy of the kitchen. Khrushchev, who at that time was expecting a visit from President Eisenhower the following year, inquired of the Waldorf what dishes the President enjoyed the most. The management researched and came up with the facts. At one point the chef noticed a salad girl preparing an avocado pear. On invitation, he tasted it, then took several up to Khrushchev's suite. Evidently Khrushchev liked it, because soon he asked for half a dozen more.

Upon finally leaving the hotel the Premier sat down to a gargantuan breakfast. He started off with a large glass of chilled orange juice, followed by poached fillet of sole, then a large minute steak, fried potatoes, cheese, bread and butter and coffee. Our State Department picked up the bill, the Russian checked out and went back to Moscow.

And speaking of unusual menus, the annual Explorers' Club Banquet, which takes place at the Waldorf, is the most interesting. The National Explorers' Club, gourmets in the strict sense of the word, manage to down what most of us would consider rather inedible cuisine. The Waldorf, however, not to be discounted when it comes to the preparation of any kind of cuisine, makes a special kitchen available to the club for their banquet. And perhaps with good reason, as we all know that cooking odors, although generally tempting, can often be dispensed with. Particularly in light of a typical menu of the Explorers' Club. At a recent meeting:

> Raw lamb's eyes,
> Two-hundred-year-old turtle eggs,
> Beaver liver,
> Roast possum,
> Wild boar,
> Chocolate-covered ants.

A pretesting by the chefs at the Waldorf is generally dispensed with at these dinners.

Heads of state are frequent visitors at the Waldorf, but captains of industry and business corporation presidents are ubiquitous. And periodically Conrad Hilton, chairman of the board of Hilton Hotels Corporation and the Hotel Waldorf-Astoria Corporation, presents a President's Dinner. The black-tie event is stag and the guests are the presidents and other distinguished executives of major companies around the country. The reception for the last one, in 1962, took place in the East Foyer, and the dinner, in the Jade Room. Following dinner, guests returned to the East Foyer, where after-dinner drinks were served and Alan King, Peter Lind Hayes, and Mary Healy entertained.

The complete Waldorf gold service—china, glassware and flatware—was used for this dinner. Always kept under lock and key, this service must all be washed by hand, being too delicate for machine washing. The china, a service for 500, is in eggshell with a 14-carat trimming in the grape design. The glassware is trimmed in gold and includes the standard glass, a 10½-ounce glass and a 2-ounce sherry glass.

Frequently, the Waldorf is called upon to entertain more than one V.I.P. simultaneously. Often, dozens of V.I.P.s are accommodated and entertained at the same time. May 23, 1963, is a case in point. Perhaps no single day in the glittering history of the hotel could have held more excitement, drama and near pandemonium. That was the day following New York's celebration in honor of astronaut Major Gordon Cooper. After the parade, which was witnessed by an estimated two million people, some two thousand prominent New Yorkers attended the luncheon given in the Major's honor in the Grand Ballroom of the Waldorf.

On the morning of the 23rd, America's newest hero and the five astronauts who preceded him in space flight were still residing in the Waldorf, although preparing for their departure. Soon, however, the scene was to become more complicated. Before midnight President Kennedy was to be honored at a fabulous dinner by some New

York friends in the Empire and Sert Rooms, with entertainment by some of America's most famous stars in the Park Avenue Foyer, closed that night to the public for the first time since the present Waldorf-Astoria was opened in 1931. At 3:30 in the afternoon the show was being rehearsed by such distinguished theater and entertainment personalities as Alan Jay Lerner, Audrey Hepburn, Carol Channing, Henry Fonda, Mitch Miller, Jimmy Durante, Eddie Fisher and Donald O'Connor. While this was in process, the carpenters were busily constructing the box where the President would sit. A small army of hotel men and maids were bustling about making preparations for the dinner. Executive Chef Eugene Scanlan was directing operations for the thousands of dinners to be served and pastry chef Willy Ritz was giving final touches to J.F.K.'s giant birthday cake and to sixty smaller cakes for guests attending the President's party.

However, not only was the President to be feted that day, but two Presidents who had preceded him as well, former Presidents Herbert Hoover and Dwight D. Eisenhower. In the afternoon, Mr. Hoover had been recipient of the 1963 Award of the Circumnavigators' Club in his suite in the Waldorf Towers. A few hours later he was called upon by President Kennedy en route to his own fete. At the same time President Eisenhower had been introduced as the speaker of the evening at a great banquet given in the Grand Ballroom by the American Iron and Steel Institute.

Meanwhile, that same day, a former King of England, the Duke of Windsor, and his American-born Duchess had arrived for an early stay in the Towers. Former Vice-President Richard M. Nixon also had checked in as had the then Vice-President Lyndon B. Johnson. While General Douglas MacArthur was quietly lunching with friends in his Towers apartment, another famed American military leader, General Mark Clark, was being honored at a Father's Day luncheon in the Grand Ballroom. And add to the list His Eminence Francis Cardinal Spellman; Earl E. T. Smith, former Ambassador to Cuba; Henry J. Taylor and Jack O'Brian, who were at a luncheon in the Empire Room to receive awards for patriotic leadership.

General and Mrs. Douglas MacArthur.

And so it went throughout the hotel, both in front of and behind the scenes. Under the capable organization of Frank G. Wangeman, executive vice-president and general manager, and Thomas J. Kane, vice-president and manager, a happy sequel was added to the star-studded day in the Waldorf's history. Everything went off with "the usual Waldorf genius," as one highly placed guest said. Conrad Hilton would have been very proud indeed.

The Waldorf, however, does not limit itself to the entertainment of people alone. On April 20, 1964, an elegant black-tie champagne party was thrown in Peacock Alley in honor of a small reddish-brown cocker spaniel with a poodle haircut. The dog's name is Jingabo, about whom the book *The Dog Who Lives at the Waldorf*, by James Brough, was written.

Peacock Alley was closed to the public for the evening and Jingabo received a parade of celebrities and socialites by "invitation only." Chef Scanlan had created a likeness of Jingabo in ice which held caviar. Jerome Zerbe, host for the evening, presented Jingabo with a solid-gold collar commemorative disc which was placed on a gold and "diamond" collar. You can spot Jingabo to this very day getting in and out of the elevator of the Waldorf Towers, where he lives.

The following autumn, on November 9, 1965, New York City and the rest of northeastern United States as well as a large section of Canada were suddenly thrown into darkness by a supposed wrench in the works near Niagara Falls. It was indeed a night to remember—the stories of the event still being batted around at cocktail parties and dinners.

And that was also the night that the Waldorf-Astoria was for the first time in its history completely bathed in the romance of candlelight. Things went surprisingly well, as a matter of fact. Both staff and guests came through with flying colors. In the famous Grand Ballroom, the closing dinner of the National Commercial Finance Conference took place by candlelight—the reception before the dinner, the menu as planned, the musicians playing, and the guest of honor speaking, presenting his address without the benefit of the microphones.

The Bull and Bear Restaurant, Peacock Alley Restaurant and the Coffee House served guests throughout the evening. The staff remained at their posts and report that the diners were wonderfully cooperative and in amazingly good spirits. With candles gleaming on every table and the kitchen ranges operated by gas, the Waldorf restaurants were able to produce almost all of the regular menu items. Even the advance supply of ice held out until after midnight. When all the dishes ran out late in the evening (the dishwasher is electric), paper plates and cups were available.

Hundreds of candles illuminated the lobby and lower floors, where stranded commuters were given refuge for the night, and employees checked the upper floors and provided candles to guests remaining in their rooms. In the morning, the Waldorf had breakfast ready.

Perhaps the one story best embodying the spirit of the evening centered around a busboy. On the fortieth floor of the Towers, a rather elegant cocktail party was in full swing. Caviar had been ordered for the guests. After a while, the ice used to chill the delicacy had melted. "Never fear," boasted the kitchen. A busboy was dispatched and, in as much time as it might take a young man to climb the forty stories, the caviar was sitting in the middle of a bucket of ice.

As a memento of the evening the Waldorf issued membership cards to all who participated. The card confers upon any present that night membership in the Waldorf-Astoria Blackout Club, "in recognition of participation and cooperation as a wonderful guest on the dark night of November 9, 1965, in New York City." The card entitles the holder to priority for seating in either the Bull and Bear or Peacock Alley on the night of the next blackout.

And, the Waldorf remembers its own, as witnessed by the annual dinner for Waldorf alumni. Hosted by Frank G. Wangeman, executive vice-president and general manager of the Waldorf-Astoria, the black-tie stag dinner is attended by men who have become hotel managers, or attained other success, after working at the Waldorf-Astoria, where many of them learned the hotel business. Last year's dinner began in the wine cellar (which is actually on the fifth floor of the hotel), where rare wines, cocktails and hors d'oeuvres were offered to the distinguished alumni. The party then took an elevator to the soup room in the main kitchen, which is on the hotel's second floor. Chefs behind the giant steam pots (50–100 gallons each) dished hot Testado Broth, a soup made of turtle and beef consommé with finely chopped vegetables, into mugs and served it to the guests. The party then proceeded to the seventeenth floor, where a buffet dinner was served at the Canadian Club (one of two private clubs located at the Waldorf). After dinner, coffee and cordials were served in the Presidential Suite on the thirty-fifth floor of the Waldorf Towers.

Often, events of historical importance take place in the Waldorf. On Monday, October 4, 1965, the historic meeting between His Holiness Pope Paul VI and President Lyndon B. Johnson took place on the thirty-fifth floor of the Waldorf-Astoria Towers. Although the Pope was not in residence at the Waldorf during his stay (he was staying at the Cardinal's residence), the hotel nonetheless was the place for the meeting and was responsible for the preparation of His Holiness' meals during the visit.

The President greeted His Holiness in the entrance foyer of 35H. The foyer has off-white walls, an oval rust rug and a large rust and gold chandelier. It is furnished with a Chippendale love seat in rust velvet, a rust and white upholstered chair, black marble-topped tables. There are two black and gold framed mirrors and three black and white prints on the walls.

The private talk between His Holiness and the President took place in the adjacent suite 35J. The furniture in this suite is English and French. The walls are white and the carpet is a bright blue bordered in a geometric design of orange and white. There is a couch of the same blue. Draperies are gold and white satin damask, over sheer white curtains, and there are chairs in matching gold and white. There is a desk between the windows and a fireplace with a mirror above it opposite the windows. Two Dresden figures were placed on the mantel. Vases of mums and roses decorated the room. Two paintings in antique gold frames were *View at Gillingham* by William James Miller and a pastoral scene by Francis Wheatley. There were also two paintings of Neapolitan scenes.

Following the private talk, His Holiness and the President went into the large drawing room of 35H for pictures. They sat in front of the fireplace banked with white rhododendron leaves on matching Chippendale chairs upholstered in rust. Two Waterford crystal candelabra with gold candles and a jade box were placed on the mantel and there were Waterford crystal lamps with brass saucer bases and white shades on fruitwood tables beside each chair. Above the mantel was Francis Remington's painting *The Love Call,* done in 1909 and now valued at $85,000. This room had white walls with a rust rug and draperies. Other appointments in the room included a French satin damask sofa, marble-topped tables, Chinese porcelain lamps and a French desk.

Chef Scanlan supervised the production of His Holiness' meals and commented, "I wished merely to please his palate." And so the luncheon prepared in the kitchens of the Waldorf and the Cardinal's residence consisted of triple-strength chicken broth with julienne of chicken, carrots and celery; scallopini of veal (two pieces to be served) with saffron rice; watercress, romaine and endive salad with an oil and lemon dressing; citron glace soufflé served with fresh fruits, berries and hot macaroons and coffee.

A luncheon such as this is always very highly organized with special instructions issued from the chef. Instructions follow.

Instructions for Serving of Luncheon
at the Cardinal's Residence in Connection
with the Visit of His Holiness Pope Paul VI
Monday, October 4th, 1965

TABLE SETTING

Dining-room table is to be set for four persons.

We will use the Cardinal's lace cloth. Luncheon napkins as selected.

FLOWERS

There will be a centerpiece of flowers—yellow and white. No candles for luncheon.

Table will be set with gold set plate.

Chicken broth will be served in consommé cup and underliner and served on the set plate.

Bread and butter plate with knife on plate.

CLEARING OF FIRST COURSE

When the consommé cup and saucer is removed, the gold set plate will also be removed.

VEAL

Very hot dinner plate. One butler will pass the veal and the second man the saffron rice.

SALAD

Salad will be served with the veal. Make sure salad plates are chilled. Salad will be mixed with dressing in salad bowl and the butler will serve the salad rather than offering it.

When the veal and salad plates have been removed, we will then serve the dessert. Hot macaroons will be presented on small compotier stand.

CAFÉ

We will be equipped for making espresso. However, inquiry will be made as to whether we will serve large coffee, demitasse or espresso.

FINGER BOWLS

Finger bowls are to be served with lukewarm water and yellow rose petals. Be certain that lemon is available with this service.

All china, glassware and silver as selected will be used.

In clearing, particularly His Holiness' china, glassware and silver as well as napkin, it is to be handled as per my special instructions.

Bread and rolls as ordered by Chef Scanlan. Special roll will be on bread and butter plate when table is set.

BEVERAGES

We will offer a choice of either red wine or white wine. This will also be immediately following the service of the veal. Poland water is to be used.

The dinner which was served that evening included:

Double Strength Beef Broth with Quenelles of Beef
* * *
Whole Completely Boned Baby Chicken
Stuffed with Wild Rice and Foie Gras
Fresh String Beans Sautéed with Mushrooms
* * *
Center of White Leaves of Boston Lettuce
Special Dressing
* * *
Cheese Tray with Port au Salut, Brie and Wisconsin Edam
To Be Passed Separately and Served with the Fresh Fruits.
* * *
Fresh Fruits Consisting of
Pears, Apples, Grapes, Cherries and Marshall Strawberries.
Petits Fours
Demitasse

*Instructions for Serving of Dinner at the Cardinal's
Residence in Connection with the Visit of His Holiness
Pope Paul VI, Monday, October 4th, 1965*

DINNER

All china as selected.

The beef broth will be served in soup plate with underliner, which will be served similar to the luncheon.

Follow instructions on clearing as for luncheon.

CHICKEN

Be certain that the dinner plates are very hot.

Butler #1 will pass the chickens and Butler #2 the stringbeans sautéed with mushrooms.

The salad is to be served as a separate course. Make sure salad plates are chilled.

When salad is removed we will then present fresh fruit in special silver baskets. We will then serve the china as selected.

It will also be necessary to have a bread and butter plate as well as a butter knife.

When Butler #1 is passing the cheese tray, Butler #2 will offer special French bread.

Be certain that the grape scissors are available as well as finger bowls.

Be certain that fruit knife is also used at each place.

GLASS SETTING

Water glass and two wine glasses.

With the chicken we will offer a choice of red or white wine.

With the cheese we will offer red wine.

Cognac will be offered with the demitasse.

All china, glassware and silver as selected will be used.

LINEN

Large dinner napkin as selected.

BEVERAGES

Be sure the champagne is chilled and available if requested by His Eminence.

The following spring, on May 14, 1966, another dignitary of the cloth was honored at the Waldorf-Astoria. The late Francis Cardinal Spellman was feted at a dinner in the Grand Ballroom. The event marked the fiftieth anniversary of his ordination. It is interesting to note just how much food, silver and china went into the presentation of this, the largest dinner ever to be held in the history of the hotel.

There was consumed:

1,800 whole tomatoes
600 pounds of fresh halibut
40 pounds of salmon roe caviar
100 live Maine lobsters for the soup

3,600 pounds of filet of prime beef
1,500 pounds of potatoes
900 pounds of asparagus
200 gallons of ice cream
260 pounds of petits fours
75 pounds of coffee to make 150 gallons of same
120 pounds of butter.

As for the china:

5,000 bread and butter plates
15,000 salad plates
5,000 soup plates
11,500 dinner plates
5,000 demitasse cups
5,000 demitasse saucers
500 Mexican bowls
1,300 raviers
1,500 ashtrays.

And in gold china:

100 bread and butter plates
300 salad plates
100 soup plates
210 dinner plates
100 demitasse cups
100 demitasse saucers
15 raviers

The glassware used that evening:

5,000 champagne saucers
500 sugar bowls
5,000 high-ball glasses
2,000 Old-Fashioned glasses
2,500 wine glasses
1,500 cocktail glasses
1,000 shot glasses
300 Tom Collins glasses

500 whiskey-sour glasses
800 salt and pepper spills
And the silver:
12 candelabra
500 soup tureens
1,000 Escoffier dishes
1,000 Escoffier dish covers
500 compotiers
2,000 assorted trays
500 coffee pots
500 table stands
And the flatware:
5,000 fish forks
7,000 dinner forks
5,000 soup spoons
11,000 teaspoons
2,500 service spoons
5,000 bread and butter knives
5,000 dinner knives
And finally the linen:
525 tablecloths
5,000 napkins
500 side towels
150 lace tablecloths.

The dinner was attended by some 5,000 of New York City's most distinguished citizens.

And so to this day, celebrities, presidents, kings, movie stars, millionaires and everyone else continue to pass through the doors of the Waldorf-Astoria. And the stories constantly add to the legend of the great hotel.

And, as the legend grows, the reputation which the Waldorf-Astoria holds as one of the finest hotels on earth grows, also. And well it might. After all, it is the "Unofficial Palace of New York City."

PART TWO

Waldorf=Astoria Recipes

Arno Schmidt, Executive Chef of The Waldorf-Astoria, and Eugene R. Scanlan, Vice President and Manager.

Hors d'Oeuvres and Appetizers

Antipasto of Diced Cooked Vegetables
in Shell

1 cup finely diced crisp-cooked
  beets
1 cup finely diced crisp-cooked
  carrots
1 cup cooked green peas
1 cup finely diced celery
1/4 cup minced green onion
1/2 cup finely diced fresh mushrooms (raw)
1/2 cup finely diced baked ham
1 cup mayonnaise
1 tablespoon mild mustard
1 tablespoon lemon juice
Salt
Pepper
Individual scallop shells

Combine vegetables and ham in large bowl. Mix mayonnaise with mustard and lemon juice. Add to vegetable-ham mixture. Season lightly with salt and pepper. Cover bowl and refrigerate for one hour or longer to allow flavors to mellow. Spoon into scallop shells to serve.

SERVES: 8.

Pâté de Foie Gras in Gelée

1 envelope unflavored gelatin
2 cups clear beef stock (or canned
  bouillon)
Salt to taste
1 egg white
2 tablespoons Madeira
6 thick slices of pâté de foie gras

Sprinkle gelatin over ½ cup of the stock in top of double boiler. Stir over hot water until dissolved. Season the remaining broth with salt if needed and stir in the dissolved gelatin.

Beat the egg white until frothy and add it to the broth. Place over moderate heat and cook, stirring until mixture boils up in the pan. Remove from heat and set aside without stirring for 10 minutes. Line a fine sieve with a triple thickness of cheesecloth which has been wrung out in cold water. Place sieve over a large bowl and strain the gelatin mixture through it. Add the Madeira and pour into a lightly greased shallow pan. Refrigerate until firm.

To serve: cut the firm gelatin into small dice. Place on individual small serving plates and place a slice of pâté de foie gras in the center of each.

SERVES: 6.

Quiche Lorraine

1 10-inch unbaked pie shell, made from rich pastry dough
5 slices of crisp-cooked bacon, crumbled
3/4 cup finely chopped Swiss cheese

2 cups rich milk
3/4 cup heavy cream
6 eggs, lightly beaten
1/4 teaspoon salt
1/4 teaspoon nutmeg
1 tablespoon grated Parmesan cheese

Prick pie shell well with a fork, line with foil and fill with dried beans. Place in preheated 375°F. oven for 6 to 8 minutes. Remove from oven and cool.

Distribute bacon and cheese evenly over bottom of pie shell.

Combine milk and cream with beaten eggs, salt and nutmeg. Blend well. Pour this mixture over the bacon and cheese.

Sprinkle surface of quiche with grated Parmesan cheese and place in preheated 375°F. oven. Bake until custard has set, 35 to 40 minutes. Serve warm.

MAKES: 1 10-inch quiche.

QUICHE SALADIER

Substitute ¼ cup chopped leeks and ¼ cup black-olive slivers for bacon.

QUICHE FLORENTINE

Substitute ¼ cup well-drained, chopped cooked spinach and 6 to 8 chopped, well-drained anchovy fillets for bacon.

QUICHE MILANO

Substitute one small seeded and chopped tomato, ¼ cup minced salami for bacon.

QUICHE TYROLIENNE

Substitute ¼ cup chopped onion, ¼ cup chopped fresh mushrooms for bacon.

QUICHE À L'AMÉRICAINE

Substitute ¼ cup chopped cooked lobster for bacon.

Escargots Bourguignons

1/4 pound salted butter at room temperature
1/2 clove garlic, minced
1 teaspoon freshly ground black pepper

1 teaspoon Worcestershire sauce
2 dozen canned escargots (snails) with shells

Combine butter, garlic, pepper and Worcestershire sauce. Blend until smooth.

Wash snail shells well. Drain thoroughly.

Put a little of the prepared butter in the bottom of each shell, add one escargot and cover with more butter. Set upright in a shallow baking pan so that when butter melts, it will not run out of shells.

Bake in a preheated 350°F. oven for 12 minutes. Serve piping hot.

A good accompaniment for snails is a loaf of French bread, a good green salad with garlic vinegar dressing and some fine imported cheese.

SERVES: 2 as a main course, 4 as an appetizer.

Guacamole Dip

5–6 large avocados (about 4 cups
   chopped avocado)
1 3-ounce package cream cheese
1/3 cup finely chopped green
   pepper
1/2 cup finely chopped jalapeño
   pepper

1 teaspoon Worcestershire sauce
1/4 teaspoon Tabasco sauce
Salt
Pepper } to taste
2 hard-cooked eggs, finely
   chopped

Cut avocados in half, remove seeds and skins. Chop and combine
with cream cheese. Mash until smooth. Add green pepper, jalapeño
peppers, Worcestershire and Tabasco sauce. Blend well, season to taste
with salt and pepper. Pile into a crystal bowl. Sprinkle with hard-
cooked eggs and serve.

SERVES: 6 to 8 as an appetizer.

Avocado Clam Velvet

2 large ripe avocados (2 cups
   diced)
1 cup cream
1/2 cup minced clams and liquid
1/2 cup chilled chicken stock

Lemon juice
Salt
Cayenne pepper
Minced chives

Cut avocados in half, remove seeds and skins. Dice fruit. Beat
smooth with rotary beater. Slowly beat in cream.

Blend in clams and chicken stock. Beat until smooth as velvet.
Season with a drop or two of lemon juice, salt to taste and a dash of
cayenne pepper. Pile into large serving bowl. Sprinkle surface with
chopped chives. Serve with unsalted crackers, small water biscuits or
Melba toast rounds.

MAKES: about 3½-cup dip.

Cold Hors d'Oeuvres

TOMATO AND AVOCADO BALLS WITH
THOUSAND ISLAND DIP

Plunge cherry tomatoes into boiling water, rinse under cold water and peel off skins.

Cut balls of avocado with a French ball cutter, dip in lemon juice.

Slice the top from a large green pepper, scoop out seeds and fill with Thousand Island dressing.

Spear tomatoes and avocado balls with cocktail picks, arrange on lettuce-lined serving plate, place filled green-pepper case in the center to serve as a dip.

OLIVE/CHEESE-STUFFED CELERY

Soften cream cheese with a little mayonnaise; add minced ripe or stuffed olives; season to taste with minced onion, salt and pepper. Fill crisp, tender stalks of celery with the mixture and dust with paprika. Or blend cream cheese with Roquefort cheese, moisten with a little cream, and season to taste. Fill celery stalks with the mixture.

AVOCADO-STUFFED CELERY (LOS ANGELES)

Mash avocado, and season well with lemon juice, salt and a dash of grated onion. Stuff celery stalks with the mixture and dust lightly with paprika.

Cornets of Smoked Salmon
with Cream Horseradish Filling

1 cup sour cream
4 tablespoons fresh horseradish

8 thin slices of smoked salmon
Thin lemon wedges

Combine sour cream and horseradish. Blend well. Refrigerate until well chilled. Cut salmon slices into 2-inch squares. Fold from corner to corner to form small cornets. Spear each with cocktail pick to hold firmly together. Place chilled sour cream and horseradish in a pastry bag and fill each cornet with the mixture. Refrigerate again until well chilled. Serve garnished with thin wedges of lemon.

MAKES: 4 to 6 servings as an appetizer.

Artichoke and Crab Cocktail

1 cup lump crabmeat
1/2 cup heavy cream, whipped
1 cup mayonnaise
1/2 cup tomato catsup
1/2 teaspoon Worcestershire sauce
1 tablespoon lemon juice

1 teaspoon grated onion
Salt to taste
1 1/2 cups diced cooked
   artichoke hearts
Lemon wedges

Pick over crabmeat to remove pieces of shell.

Blend whipped cream with mayonnaise, catsup and seasonings. Mix lightly with artichoke hearts and crabmeat. Chill thoroughly. Serve in lettuce-lined cocktail glasses, garnished with wedges of lemon.

MAKES: 8 servings.

Canapé Trianon

3 slices white bread
Butter
3 thin slices of smoked sturgeon,
   size of bread

3 thin slices Nova Scotia salmon,
   a little smaller than the sturgeon
   slices
3 teaspoons caviar

Toast bread, trim off crust and spread lightly with butter. Cover each slice, first with sturgeon then with salmon. Cut each into four small squares. Top each square with ¼ teaspoon caviar.

MAKES: 12 hors d'oeuvres.

Monte Cristo Sandwich

For each sandwich:

2 slices white bread
Butter at room temperature
1 thin slice baked or boiled ham
1 thin slice Swiss cheese
1 thin slice baked or boiled white meat of chicken

1 thin slice American cheese
1 egg
Dash of salt
1 tablespoon cold water
1 tablespoon salad oil
Butter and oil for frying

Spread both bread slices with butter. Place ham on one slice, top with Swiss cheese, add chicken, then American cheese. Cover with second slice of bread. Press sandwich firmly together. Wrap prepared sandwich in damp cold napkin (sprinkle napkin with ice water, wring damp dry). Refrigerate until well chilled or until ready to cook.

Combine egg, salt, pepper, cold water and salad oil in small bowl. Blend well with wire whisk. Pour into shallow pan or dish with rim.

Holding sandwich firmly together, dip it in this mixture, first on one side, then the other.

Fry sandwich in heavy skillet in ⅔ cooking oil, ⅓ butter (sufficient to cover bottom of skillet to ⅛ inch). When browned on both sides, remove from skillet and transfer to a shallow baking dish. Place in preheated 350°F. oven for 8 to 10 minutes.

Allow sandwich to cool a few moments, then drain briefly on paper toweling before serving.

Slice sandwich in half and serve as luncheon entrée.

Remove crust, cut into four small squares. Serve as a late snack.

Remove crust, cut into four "fingers." Cut fingers in half and serve as hors d'oeuvres.

Green Turtle Soup

7 *cups clear beef consommé*
1 *teaspoon turtle herbs (may be*
   purchased in gourmet food
   shops)

1/2 *cup sherry*
1 *teaspoon arrowroot*
1/2 *cup diced turtle meat*
   (canned)

Combine 1 cup of the consommé with the turtle herbs in a large saucepan. Place over low heat and allow to simmer very gently for 10 minutes.

Combine sherry and arrowroot, blend and add to simmering consommé. Add remaining consommé and turtle meat. Heat thoroughly and serve.

SERVES: 6 to 8.

Black Bean Soup

2 *pounds dried black beans*
4 *tablespoons sweet butter*
1 *large onion, finely chopped*
2 *medium carrots, finely chopped*
3 *quarts water*
1 *teaspoon salt*

3 *tablespoons butter*
2 *tablespoons flour*

3 *cups chicken stock or broth*
1 *cup milk*

1 *cup heavy cream*
2 *tablespoons sweet butter*
Salt
Freshly ground black }*to taste*
   pepper
1 *hard-cooked egg, finely chopped*

Pick over and wash beans. Cover with water and soak overnight.

Place butter, onion and carrots in large soup kettle, sauté until tender—do not allow to brown.

Drain and add beans to kettle. Add cooking water and salt. Bring to boil, lower heat and allow to simmer gently about three hours or until beans are tender. Put through a sieve or purée in an electric blender.

Melt the three tablespoons of butter in a saucepan. Add flour and stir over low heat until smooth. Slowly stir in the chicken stock or broth and milk. Cook, stirring, over moderate heat until mixture thickens slightly. Combine with puréed beans in soup kettle, bring to boil, stirring constantly. Add remaining ingredients except chopped egg. Continue cooking only until soup is again very hot. Do not allow to boil after adding cream. Add chopped egg, ladle into bowls and serve.

SERVES: 8–12.

Cold Senegalese Soup

3 1/2 cups clear chicken stock or broth, canned or homemade
1 cup finely chopped cooked chicken
1 to 2 teaspoons curry powder

4 egg yolks
2 cups light cream
Salt ⎱ to taste
Pepper ⎰
Cold cooked shredded chicken

In a saucepan, combine chicken stock, chicken and curry powder. Bring to boil, turn heat to very low and allow to simmer.

Beat yolks until light, then quickly stir in about 2 tablespoons of the hot stock. Add the cream, blend well and stir this mixture back into the stock. Cook, stirring, over low heat until soup thickens slightly. Do not allow to boil. Season to taste with salt and pepper. Refrigerate until well chilled. Garnish each serving with bits of shredded chicken.

MAKES: about 6 bowls or 12 small cups of soup.

Consommé Hilton

1 large onion, chopped	1 turnip, sliced
1 tablespoon butter	1 large onion stuck with one clove
3 pounds shoulder of beef	1 stalk of celery with leaves
1/4 pound beef marrow bones	2-3 sprigs parsley
1 veal knuckle	Small bunch chervil
1 beef knuckle	1 small parsnip, sliced
5 quarts water	2 teaspoons salt
2 carrots, sliced	6 peppercorns

Cook onion in butter over moderate heat to a deep golden brown. Set aside.

Place the meat, bones and water in a large soup kettle. Bring to boil and skim the surface until clear. Add the browned onion and remaining ingredients, lower heat, cover and allow to simmer slowly for 3 to 4 hours. Cool to room temperature. Remove the meat and bones, strain the stock into quart containers. Refrigerate until fat rises to the surface and congeals. Remove fat. Reheat and use as needed.

MAKES: about 3 quarts consommé.

NOTE: Consommé may be frozen and stored in freezer.

Clam Chowder

5 to 6 dozen chowder clams	2 tablespoons tomato purée
2 large onions, chopped	1 teaspoon thyme
4 ribs celery, chopped	3 cups potatoes, peeled and diced
4-6 leeks, chopped	Salt
1 medium green pepper, seeded and chopped	Freshly ground black pepper } to taste
1/4 pound butter	1 tablespoon Worcestershire sauce
1 1-pound can whole tomatoes and juice	

Scrub clams thoroughly under cold running water. Place in large kettle or clam steamer with ½ cup water. Steam the clams until they open, 10 to 12 minutes depending on size.

Save the liquid, remove clams from shells and remove the long necks and coarse membrane. Coarse-chop. Set aside.

Measure the liquid saved from the clams and add sufficient water to make 2 quarts liquid and set aside.

In a large soup kettle, sauté the onions, celery, leeks and green pepper in the butter until limp. Add the clam liquid, tomatoes, tomato purée, thyme and 2 cups of the diced potatoes. Bring to boil, cover, lower heat and simmer for 30 minutes.

Boil the remaining potatoes in water to cover in separate saucepan. When tender, drain, mash thoroughly and stir into the chowder. Add the clams and Worcestershire sauce. Correct seasoning with additional salt if needed. Continue cooking only until clams are thoroughly heated.

MAKES: about 3 quarts soup.

Soup au Geraumon (Pumpkin Soup)

1 pound soup meat with bones	1/4 cup minced chives
2 1/2 quarts water	1 teaspoon salt
3 small carrots, scraped and diced	1/2 teaspoon pepper
2 small turnips, peeled and diced	1/4 teaspoon thyme
2 leeks, chopped	1 teaspoon vinegar
3 large cabbage leaves, chopped	6 slices of white bread, crust re-
2 cups (canned) mashed pumpkin	moved
4 ounces vermicelli	4 tablespoons butter

Place soup meat and water in large kettle. Bring to boil and skim surface. When clear, reduce heat and add carrots, turnips, leeks and cabbage. Simmer gently 2½ to 3 hours or until meat is tender. Remove meat and set aside.

Stir pumpkin into soup. Cook, stirring frequently, for 10 to 15 minutes. Add vermicelli, chives and seasoning. Allow to simmer until vermicelli is tender.

Cut three slices of the bread into ½-inch cubes. Melt 2 tablespoons of the butter in a small saucepan. Add the bread cubes and cook over medium heat until crisp and dry. Add to the soup and allow them to be absorbed into the liquid. Stir in the remaining butter.

Cut remaining bread slices in half. Serve soup from large tureen, ladling it out into soup bowls over half slices of bread.

Serve soup meat separately.

SERVES: 8 to 12.

Fish and Shellfish

Peacock Alley

Entered through a two-story-high colonade reminiscent of the famed Brighton Pavillion of the English Regency period, Peacock Alley is a true gourmet dining pleasure.

The name "Peacock Alley" derives from the old Waldorf-Astoria, where the promenade between the two adjoining buildings was a favorite strolling place for turn-of-the-century New York society. Someone chanced to remark that the corridor where the distinguished gentlemen and their bejeweled and gowned ladies would appear on the way to or from lavish receptions and balls, seemed like an alley of peacocks.

Peacock Alley is still the restaurant where the great and near great come to preen, and everyone comes for gourmet French and Continental specialties at breakfast, luncheon, cocktails and dinner. At the entrance to Peacock Alley is a charming garden overlooking the main lobby especially popular for cocktails and people watching.

Lobster Côte d'Emeraude

2 1 1/2- to 2-pound lobsters
Boiling salted water
1/2 cup chopped shallots
3 tablespoons butter
2 cups rich tomato sauce
3 teaspoons tomato purée

1 1/2 cup Hollandaise sauce (see
   recipe, page 197)
Salt ⎫
Pepper ⎬ to taste
4 croustades (see below)
Rice pilaf (see recipe below)

Plunge the live lobsters into a large deep pan of boiling water. Cover and simmer for 5 minutes for the first pound, 3 minutes for each additional pound. Remove from water and allow to cool slightly. With a heavy knife and a mallet or hammer, split each lobster lengthwise, starting at the head. Remove and discard the stomach and intestinal vein. Remove and crack claws. Remove meat from claws and cut large pieces into bite size.

Place body halves with tail meat intact on broiler rack. Set aside.

Sauté the shallots in the butter until limp, add the tomato sauce and tomato purée. Simmer until reduced by one third. Remove from heat and add the lobster meat and ⅓ of the Hollandaise sauce. Season to taste with salt and pepper. Fill each lobster cavity with some of this stuffing (reserving about ¼ cup for the croustades). Spread lobster tails with Hollandaise sauce (reserving about 2 teaspoons for the croustades).

Place prepared lobster about 4 inches under medium broiler heat. Broil until surfaces are lightly browned. Serve at once with a mound of rice pilaf and a hot filled croustade on each plate.

SERVES: 4.

CROUSTADES

Cut the tops from four small, round crusty French rolls and remove the soft center. Spread the cavities with soft butter. Place in a preheated 400°F. oven until lightly toasted. Fill with prepared lobster filling. Spread filling with Hollandaise sauce. Place under broiler heat with lobsters 2 or 3 minutes before lobsters are ready to take from the broiler.

RICE PILAF

1 *small onion, chopped*
1 *tablespoon olive oil*
1 *tablespoon butter*
1 *cup short-grain Italian rice*

3 *cups clear chicken stock or broth*
Salt and pepper to taste
Pinch of saffron

Sauté onion in the olive oil and butter in a large saucepan until limp. Add the rice and cook, stirring, over medium heat until each grain is coated with oil.

Bring stock to a full boil in a separate saucepan. Season to taste with salt and pepper. Stir in the saffron and pour, boiling, over rice. Cover pan and simmer over low heat until rice has absorbed all liquid. Pack cooked dry rice into small baba molds and turn out onto serving plates.

Mousse of Boston Sole Nantua
with Shrimp Sauce à la Eugène

2 *pounds Boston sole*
1 *teaspoon salt*
1/4 *teaspoon white pepper*
2 *tablespoons sherry*
1/2 *teaspoon dry mustard*

4 *egg yolks, lightly beaten*
1 1/2 *cups heavy cream*
4 *egg whites*
Shrimp sauce à la Eugène (see below)

Remove all skin and bones from sole and force through the finest blade of a food chopper. Place in large mixing bowl, add salt, pepper, sherry, mustard and egg yolks. Blend well.

Beat cream until stiff. Beat egg whites until stiff. Fold beaten cream and egg whites alternately into fish mixture. Transfer to a 2½- to 3-quart well-buttered soufflé mold. Place mold in large pan of warm water and place in a preheated 350°F. oven. Bake for 25 to 30 minutes or until firm. Unmold onto heated platter. Spoon sauce over surface and serve.

SERVES: 4.

Shrimp Sauce à la Eugène

2 tablespoons butter
2 tablespoons flour
1 cup fish stock (see page 107)
1 cup light cream

2 tablespoons sherry
Salt
White pepper } to taste
1/2 cup diced cooked shrimp

Heat the butter in a saucepan. Add the flour and stir until smooth. Slowly add the fish stock, stirring it into the flour-butter mixture as it is added. Add the cream and stir over low heat until sauce thickens. Add the sherry, season to taste with salt and pepper, and add the shrimp. Continue to cook, stirring, only until shrimp are heated.

MAKES: about 2½ cups sauce.

Lobster Flambé

2 cups cooked lobster meat, large
  chunks
3 tablespoons butter
Salt

Freshly ground black pepper
1/4 cup fine Cognac or brandy
1/4 cup heavy cream

This is a very simple but delicious way to prepare lobster in a chafing dish.

Heat lobster in butter over fairly high heat. (Lobster should cook only briefly or it will become tough.) Sprinkle with salt and pepper and pour in the Cognac. Tilt the pan so that the fire "jumps into the pan" and ignites the Cognac. Let the flame burn briefly. Then spoon the flaming lobster onto serving plates. Let the flame die out in the pan, add the cream, and stir it into the Cognac and butter. Heat briefly (do not allow to boil, however, after adding cream). Pour some of this sauce over each serving of lobster and serve at once.

SERVES: 2.

NOTE: An excellent accompaniment to lobster flambé is wild rice.

Shrimp in Nantua Sauce

1 1/2-pound live lobster	1 1/4-inch piece bay leaf
1/2 cup olive oil	Beurre manié—of 2 tablesoons
1 clove garlic, chopped	flour creamed with 2 tablespoons
1 large onion, chopped	butter
2 stalks celery, chopped	
1 smal carrot, scraped and	1 pound small shrimp, shelled and
chopped	deveined
5 cups thin fish stock (see below)	1 cup sherry wine
1 cup tomato purée	1 cup heavy cream
1 teaspoon anise seed	Salt
1/8 teaspoon curry powder	Pepper } to taste

Place lobster on its back on a wooden board and quickly split lengthwise. Remove and discard small sac below head. Remove and discard intestinal vein running down center of body. Crack claws and cut lobster tail into thick slices. Break up body into large pieces.

Heat oil in a deep heavy skillet, add the lobster and cook over moderately high heat, turning the pieces often, until shells are red on all sides. Add garlic, onion, celery and carrot. Cook, stirring, until onion is transparent. Add stock, tomato purée, anise seed and curry. Cover and allow to simmer for about 20 minutes; add bay leaf the last 5 minutes. Add the beurre manié and stir until well blended into the sauce. Remove from heat. Remove lobster and take meat from shells. Place in electric blender and blend to a smooth paste. Strain sauce and add puréed lobster.

Combine shrimp and wine in second large saucepan. Cook over medium heat until shrimps turn pink (about 5 minutes). Add lobster sauce and cream. Season to taste with salt and pepper. Cook, stirring gently, until all ingredients are thoroughly heated. Do not allow to boil after adding cream. Serve at once over freshly made hot rice or over hot toast points.

SERVES: 4.

FISH STOCK

2 *pounds bones, heads, skin and trimmings from flounder, sole, whiting, etc.*	1 *bay leaf*
1 *onion, chopped*	1 *teaspoon salt*
1 *carrot, scraped and chopped*	8–10 *peppercorns*
3–4 *sprigs parsley*	5 *cups water*
	1 *cup dry white wine*
	1/4 *teaspoon salt*

Combine ingredients in large saucepan, bring to boil. Lower heat and allow to simmer gently for about 30 minutes. Strain. Refrigerate and use as needed.

If stock is not used within one week, reheat and refrigerate for a second week. Repeat weekly until used.

Shrimp à la Captain John
on Garlic Toast

5 *tablespoons butter*	*Salt*
1 *teaspoon minced garlic*	*Freshly ground black* } *to taste*
1/2 *cup chopped shallots*	*pepper*
2 *cups stewed (canned) tomatoes*	2 *dozen large cooked fresh shrimp*
	2 *slices white bread*

107

Cream 1 tablespoon of the butter with half of the minced garlic. Set aside at room temperature. Do not allow to melt.

Sauté the remaining garlic and the shallots in 2 tablespoons of the butter in a large saucepan. When limp, add the tomatoes and cook, stirring frequently, over low heat to a thick sauce. Season with salt and pepper to taste. Keep hot.

Melt the remaining butter in a second saucepan. Add the shrimp and stir, only until they are heated. Add the tomato sauce and blend well.

Remove crust from bread and cut in half. Spread with garlic butter. Place in a 400°F. oven until lightly toasted.

Spoon sauce and shrimp over hot toast and serve at once.

SERVES: 2.

Long Island Striped Bass Belle Meunière
(Princess Margaret Dinner)

1 5- to 6-pound bass	*String to tie bass*
1 cup chopped cooked spinach, well drained	*Oil*
	1 cup milk
1/4 cup chopped anchovy fillets, drained	*1/2 cup flour*
	1/2 cup butter
1 egg yolk	*Salt*
Pepper	*Thin lemon slices*

Have the fish dealer clean the bass, split it and remove the bones without detaching the halves.

Combine the spinach, anchovy fillets and egg yolks; season with pepper. Blend well and spoon into cavity of fish.

Place sufficient string to tie fish together in oil. Let soak for 5 to 10 minutes.

Place milk in shallow pan. Place flour on waxed paper. Dip fish gently in milk, then roll in flour. Dust off excess flour and tie body together with the oil-soaked string.

Heat the butter in an ovenproof skillet—one large enough to hold the fish without crowding—add the fish and quickly brown on both sides. Transfer skillet to a preheated 375°F. oven and bake the fish until the flesh flakes easily with a fork, 20 to 25 minutes.

Remove string, sprinkle surface of fish with salt and serve garnished with thin slices of lemon.

SERVES: 4.

Cold Salmon with Wine Aspic

1 4-pound piece of salmon	1/2 cup cold water
1 quart water	1 1/4 cups dry white wine
1/2 cup vinegar	Pimiento halves
1 onion, quartered	Hard-cooked egg slices
1 slice of lemon	Ripe olive slivers
1 bay leaf	Parsley
1 teaspoon salt	Lemon slices and wedges
1 envelope unflavored gelatin	

Wipe salmon with a damp cloth. Combine water and vinegar in large kettle; add onion, lemon slices, bay leaf and salt. Bring to boil, lower heat and allow to simmer very gently for 15 minutes. Add the salmon and poach very gently for 30 to 40 minutes. Remove from heat and allow to cool in the broth.

Remove from broth; when cool, wrap in foil or plastic wrap. Refrigerate until well chilled.

Sprinkle gelatin over the cold water in top of double boiler. Place over hot water and stir until dissolved. Add wine, remove from heat and refrigerate until of egg-white consistency.

Place fish on serving platter and brush with the slightly thickened gelatin mixture. Arrange pimiento halves over surface. Place a hard-cooked egg slice on each pimiento. Pour aspic again over surface. Refrigerate until ready to serve.

Just before serving, garnish platter with ripe-olive slivers, parsley, lemon slices and wedges.

SERVES: 6 as an entree or 8–10 as an appetizer.

Bouillabaisse Marseillaise

2 1 1/2-pound lobsters	1 bay leaf, crumbled
1 pound mackerel	Pinch of saffron
1 pound striped bass	Pinch of thyme
1 pound eel	1 teaspoon salt
3–4 Dungeness crab	1/2 tablespoon freshly ground
1 pound mussels	black pepper
3 leeks, chopped	1/2 cup olive oil
2 large onions, chopped	1 pint dry white wine
3 large tomatoes, chopped	Water
2 sprigs parsley, chopped	French bread

Have your fish dealer split and clean the lobsters.

Cut fish into 1- to 1½-inch slices. Cut lobster and eel into pieces of about the same size. Have your fish dealer clean the crabs, remove their backs, crack the claws, and cut each in half.

Wash the mussels and remove the beard (the gathering of vegetation on the shell).

Place the leeks, onions, tomatoes and parsley in the bottom of a large heavy kettle. Sprinkle seasoning over surface. Arrange the lobster, fish and crab over the vegetables. Pour the oil and wine over them and add enough water to completely cover. Bring to boil over high heat and allow to boil 12 to 15 minutes. Add the mussels and cook until they open.

Serve in soup bowls with crusty French bread to "go with."

SERVES: 6 to 8.

Bay Shrimp Newburg

1 tablespoon butter
1 pound bay shrimp, shelled and
deveined
1 tablespoon chopped shallots
1 cup dry sherry
1/2 cup cream

Beurre manié—of 1 tablespoon
butter blended with 1 teaspoon
flour
Salt }
Pepper } *to taste*

Melt the butter in a saucepan. Add the shrimp and sauté 3 to 4 minutes. Add shallots, ½ cup of the sherry and the cream. Cover and cook over low heat for 15 to 20 minutes. Stir occasionally. Remove the shrimp and cook the sauce, stirring, over medium heat until reduced to ⅓ its original quantity. Thicken by adding the beurre manié (blended butter and flour). Add the remaining ½ cup sherry, season to taste with salt and pepper. Remove from heat and strain the sauce through a fine sieve. Add reserved shrimp. Reheat briefly. Serve over toast points or white rice.

SERVES: 4.

NOTE: If sauce is overthick, thin it with a little additional sherry.

Crabmeat Remick

1 pound lump crabmeat, fresh or
canned, well picked over
1/2 cup dry white wine
1/2 teaspoon dry mustard
1/2 teaspoon paprika
1/2 teaspoon pepper
1/2 teaspoon celery salt
1/2 teaspoon Worcestershire sauce

1/2 teaspoon tarragon vinegar
1/2 teaspoon lemon juice
Dash of Tabasco sauce
1 cup prepared mayonnaise
1 cup chili sauce
2 tablespoons grated Parmesan
cheese

Pile crabmeat into six individual shells or ramekins. Sprinkle with wine.

Combine remaining ingredients, except grated cheese, in mixing bowl. Blend well.

Place crabmeat about 1 inch directly under broiler heat for one minute. Remove from oven and spread sauce mixture over surface. Sprinkle with grated cheese. Place in a preheated 375°F. oven for five minutes, then transfer to 3 inches under high broiler heat until surface is lightly browned. Serve at once.

SERVES: 6.

Filet of Sole Monterey

1 medium onion, sliced	2 tablespoons chopped shallots or green onion
2–3 sprigs parsley	
1 teaspoon salt	1 dozen small oysters
12 whole white peppercorns	
2 quarts water	1 cup heavy cream
	1/2 cup chicken stock or broth
6 sole filets	1/2 cup California Sauterne
1/4 cup butter	6 small cooked shrimp, peeled,
1/4 pound mushrooms, sliced	deveined and coarsely chopped

Combine first 5 ingredients in large saucepan. Bring to boil. Reduce heat and simmer 30 minutes. Add filets, lowering them carefully into the stock. Cook over low heat ten minutes. Remove with slotted spatula, again being careful that filets do not break or fall apart. Transfer to shallow ovenproof dish. Set aside.

Melt butter in a second saucepan. Add the mushrooms and shallots. Sauté two to three minutes. Add oysters. Cook a final minute. Set aside.

Heat cream in top of double boiler over hot water (do not allow to boil). Add chicken stock and wine. Heat thoroughly.

Place shrimp, sautéed mushrooms and oysters around fish in baking dish. Pour sauce over surface. Bake in a preheated 350°F. oven for 20 minutes. Serve at once.

SERVES: 6.

Broiled Scampi Marinara

2 pounds large unshelled raw
    shrimp, about 16 to 20 shrimp
1 cup sweet vermouth
Salt
3/4 to 1 cup olive oil

Paprika
3 tablespoons butter
1 clove garlic
Freshly boiled white rice

Peel and devein the shrimp, leaving the tails attached. Split down the inside lengthwise, being careful not to cut through the shrimp. Spread out to form butterfly shape. Place in nonmetal bowl. Add vermouth. Marinate 1 to 2 hours.

Remove shrimp from vermouth. Sprinkle with salt, dip in olive oil and dust with paprika. Broil under medium flame 7 minutes.

Melt butter with garlic in small saucepan. Cook over low heat until lightly browned. Remove garlic. Place broiled shrimp on a bed of hot, freshly boiled white rice. Pour browned butter over surface. Serve at once.

If preferred, serve on freshly made hot toast accompanied by a broiled tomato half.

SERVES: 4 to 6.

Baked Oysters Provençale

24 *bluepoint oysters*
1/4 *pound butter at room*
  temperature
1 *clove garlic, minced*
1/4 *teaspoon freshly ground black*
  pepper

1/4 *teaspoon salt*
1 *tablespoon tomato purée*
1/3 *cup Parmesan cheese*
2/3 *cup fine dry bread crumbs*

Buy oysters in the shell. Have your fish man shuck them and give you the deeper half of each shell. Wash shells well.

Combine butter, garlic, pepper, salt and tomato purée. Blend until smooth. Refrigerate until firm enough to spread.

Place an oyster in each half shell. Cover with blended butter, sprinkle with cheese and bread crumbs.

Bake in preheated 350°F. oven on rack for 15 minutes. Serve at once.

SERVES: 6.

Cauliflower Seafood Casserole

1 *large cauliflower*
Water
Salt

2 *tablespoons butter*
2 *tablespoons flour*

1 *cup milk*
1/2 *teaspoon salt*
1 *cup lump crabmeat*
1 *teaspoon lemon juice*
1/4 *cup grated Parmesan cheese*
1/4 *cup fine dry bread crumbs*

Separate cauliflower into flowerets. Cook in boiling salted water for 10 minutes. Drain thoroughly.

Melt butter in saucepan. Stir in flour; when bubbly, slowly add milk. Season with salt; stir over moderate heat until mixture thickens. Add crabmeat and lemon juice. Blend and remove from heat.

Place cauliflower flowerets in shallow baking dish and cover with crabmeat mixture. Sprinkle surface with grated cheese and bread crumbs. Place in preheated 350°F. oven and bake for 20 minutes.

SERVES: 6.

Frogs' Legs Provençale

12 pairs frogs' legs
1 cup milk
Flour
Salt
1 tablespoon butter
3 tablespoons cooking oil

3 large tomatoes, peeled, seeded, cut in quarters

1/3 cup butter
1 clove garlic, chopped
3/4 teaspoon salt
3/4 teaspoon sugar
Freshly ground black pepper to taste

Soak frogs' legs in milk for 30 minutes. Remove from milk, lightly dredge with flour and sprinkle with salt.

Heat the butter and oil in a heavy skillet. Add the frogs' legs, brown them on all sides. Cook over medium heat for 7 to 8 minutes. Drain on paper toweling to remove excess oil, then place in a shallow baking dish. Keep warm.

Dice tomatoes. Place with butter, garlic, salt and sugar in small saucepan. Cook over medium heat for 4 to 5 minutes. Chop tomatoes as they cook with a knife or the tip of a spatula. Season with pepper to taste. Pour over frogs' legs in baking dish. Place in preheated 350°F. oven for 5 minutes. Serve from baking dish if desired.

SERVES: 4.

Filet of Sole Sauté Amandine

6 sole filets	Juice from one lemon
All-purpose flour	2 tablespoons chopped parsley
1/2 cup butter	1/4 cup slivered almonds
Salt	Thin lemon wedges
Pepper	

Wash filets, wipe dry and dredge with flour. Heat one half of the butter in a large heavy skillet. Add the filets and sauté in foaming butter (medium heat) until golden brown on both sides. Remove to a warm serving platter. Sprinkle with salt and pepper.

Add the remaining butter to the skillet and let it cook over medium heat until lightly browned. Stir in the lemon juice, parsley and almonds. Blend and pour over the filets.

Garnish with thin lemon slices and serve.

SERVES: 6.

Avocado Coquille Medley

6 tablespoons butter	1/4 pound shrimp, shelled and deveined
4 tablespoons flour	
2 1/2 cups light cream	2 tablespoons dry sherry
1/4 teaspoon salt	2 tablespoons finely chopped parsley
1/2 teaspoon marjoram, crushed	
Sprinkling of pepper	4 medium avocados
3/4 pound scallops, halved or quartered	Lemon juice
	24 tarragon toast triangles (see page 117)

Melt four tablespoons of the butter in top half of a double boiler. Add flour, and blend until smooth. Slowly stir in cream, season with salt, marjoram and pepper. Stir over simmering water until sauce thickens. Keep warm over hot water.

Melt remaining butter in a large skillet, add scallops and shrimp; sook, stirring frequently, over medium heat until seafood is tender—about five minutes. Remove from heat. Add sherry and parsley, blend. Add mixture to white sauce.

Cut avocados in half lengthwise, remove seed and peel. Cut each half into thin slices. Sprinkle with lemon juice.

Spoon seafood mixture over tarragon toast slices in individual casseroles. Top with avocado slices and garnish with additional tarragon toast triangles.

SERVES: 6.

TARRAGON TOAST TRIANGLES

1/4 cup butter at room tempera-   *1/2 teaspoon crushed tarragon*
ture   *6 slices white bread*

Combine butter and tarragon. Spread on bread slices. Place in 400°F. oven until golden. Cut each diagonally into four small triangles.

Shad Roe with Sorrel

1 onion, thinly sliced   *1/2 cup dry white wine*
1/2 cup chopped shallots   *1/2 tablespoon chopped sorrel*
1 tablespoon butter   *(fresh or canned)*
2 shad roe

Sauté onion and shallots in butter until soft. Transfer to a heavy ovenproof saucepan. Place the shad roe over the vegetables, pour wine over the surface and allow to marinate for 2 hours. Bring to boil on top of the stove, sprinkle with sorrel, then cover and place in a preheated 300°F. oven for one hour. Remove the roe to a heated platter or serving plates. Reduce the cooking liquid over a medium-high heat on top of the stove until of the consistency of a thick syrup. Pour over the roe and serve.

SERVES: 2.

Coquille St. Jacques

4 tablespoons butter
1/4 pound mushrooms, thinly
   sliced
2 tablespoons finely chopped
   shallots
2 tablespoons flour
1 1/2 pounds scallops, sliced

1 1/2 cups dry white wine
1/4 teaspoon salt
1/8 teaspoon pepper
2 egg yolks, lightly beaten with 1
   tablespoon hot water
1 cup heavy cream

Melt 2 tablespoons of the butter in a saucepan, add the mushrooms and sauté for 3 to 4 minutes. Add the shallots and cook, stirring, 1 minute longer. Stir in the flour and blend until smooth. Remove from heat, set aside.

Cook the scallops in the remaining butter in a separate saucepan until tender. Remove scallops, set aside and add the wine to the juices in the pan. Bring to boil and stir into the mushroom mixture. Add salt and pepper. Cook, stirring, over moderate heat until sauce thickens. Remove from heat. Combine egg yolks and cream. Stir into sauce. Add scallops, and blend well. Spoon mixture into scallop shells or small ramekins, and place on baking sheet under medium broiler heat. Broil until surfaces are lightly browned. Serve at once.

SERVES: 6.

Grilled Filet of Sole with Anchovy Strips and Parsley Butter

1/2 cup butter at room temperature
Juice of half a lemon
1 teaspoon Worcestershire sauce
1 tablespoon finely chopped
   parsley

8 3 1/2- to 4-ounce sole filets
Cooking oil
Salt
Pepper
Fine dry bread crumbs
8 anchovy filets, cut in half

Blend soft butter with lemon juice, Worcestershire sauce and parsley. Refrigerate until firm enough to form into small "log" or roll. Wrap roll in wax paper and refrigerate until ready to prepare fish.

Brush sole with oil, sprinkle with salt and pepper and lightly dust with bread crumbs. Place on greased foil in shallow pan about 3 inches directly under broiler flame. Broil, turning once, until filets are lightly browned on both sides and flesh flakes easily with a fork. Transfer to heated serving platter or plates.

Place 2 anchovy-filet halves over each piece of fish. Top each with several thin slices of the prepared butter.

While the sole is being served, the butter will melt into the fish and give a wonderful flavor. It will also bring out the true flavor of the fish.

SERVES: 4.

Coquille of King Crabmeat Favorite

1 pound king crabmeat, diced
1 cup French dressing (see page 195)
1 1/2 cups prepared mayonnaise
1 teaspoon prepared English mustard

2 cups shredded Boston lettuce
1 hard-cooked egg, finely chopped
1 tablespoon chopped parsley
Pimiento strips

Combine crabmeat and French dressing in nonmetal bowl. Refrigerate covered 2 to 3 hours.

Drain crabmeat. Reserve French dressing.

Mix 1 cup of the mayonnaise with 2 tablespoons of the French dressing and the mustard. Add crabmeat, blend well, and pile into four attractive fish shells.

Toss lettuce with 2 tablespoons of the French dressing.

Place crab-filled shells on 4 individual salad plates. Surround with lettuce. Sprinkle with chopped egg and parsley. Garnish with thin strips of pimiento.

Blend remaining mayonnaise with remaining French dressing. Serve separately.

SERVES: 4

Terrapin

Drop a cow terrapin headfirst into boiling water and boil for 2 minutes, or until the outer skin and toenails can be removed. Then plunge it into fresh boiling salted water to cook until the shells part easily and the leg meat is tender. The portion of the joint between the upper and lower shells will show a ragged break at the joining. Lay the terrapin on its back, remove the lower shell, and cool. Remove lungs, sand bag, bladder and entrails and discard the gall sac bedded in the liver, being careful not to break it. Save the liquid in the upper shell, the eggs, and the liver. Cut the meat into pieces ½ inch long and remove the larger bones. Heat in a double boiler with the liquid from the shell, add water to cover and cook for 1½ hours or until the meat is tender. The stock will be reduced by half.

The Waldorf Astoria is world-famous for this recipe.

Chicken and Other Birds

Wiener Backhendl

3 2 1/2-pound frying chickens,
  each cut in half
1 teaspoon salt
1 cup flour
Egg wash—of 3 eggs beaten with
  1/4 cup water

2 1/2 cups fine dry bread
  crumbs
Oil for deep-frying
1 lemon, sliced

Sprinkle chicken halves with salt, dredge with flour, dip in egg wash. Let stand 5 minutes, then coat with bread crumbs.

Fill a large, heavy pan with cooking oil to 3 or 4 inches from rim. Heat to 350°F. on deep-fat thermometer (or until small cube of soft bread will brown in 35 seconds). Lower chicken pieces gently into hot fat to avoid shaking off crust. Fry to a light golden brown. Remove from pan, drain off excess fat and place in shallow baking pan.

Bake in preheated 400°F. oven for about 5 minutes or until crust is firm and deeply browned. Lower temperature to 325°F. and continue baking until chicken is thoroughly done, about 30 to 35 minutes.

Garnish each half chicken with thin lemon slice.

SERVES: 6.

Browned Chicken Fricassee

3/4 pound ground beef, chuck
1 teaspoon grated onion
1 slice white bread
1/4 cup milk
1 egg, slightly beaten
1/2 teaspoon salt
1/4 teaspoon pepper

1 frying chicken—about 2 1/2
  pounds cut into serving pieces
Salt
Freshly ground black pepper
1/2 teaspoon paprika

2 chicken breasts, cut into bite-size
  cubes
2 tablespoons butter
3 tablespoons vegetable oil
2 medium onions, chopped
1 clove garlic minced
2 1/2 cups chicken stock or broth
  (canned or homemade)
Beurre mainé—2 teasoons flour
  blended with 1 teaspoon butter

Combine ground beef and onion. Soak bread in milk, mash and add to meat. Add egg, blend well, season with salt and pepper. Shape into 12 small balls. Set aside.

Sauté chicken pieces in butter and oil in large, heavy saucepan until each piece is lightly browned. Add chicken breasts, onion and garlic. Cook, stirring frequently, until breasts turn white. Add stock, blend and add meat balls. Season with salt and pepper to taste. Stir in paprika. Cover and cook over low heat, stirring occasionally, for 45 minutes, or until chicken pieces are tender. Add beurre manié. Cook, stirring gently, only until sauce thickens. Correct seasoning with salt if needed and serve.

SERVES: 6 to 8.

Boneless Breast of Duckling
Sautéed in Cointreau and Herbs

To prepare this dish you will need to roast the whole duck. However, that portion not used may be refrigerated or frozen to be served in another way at a later date.

1 5- to 6-pound duck	*1/4 teaspoon oregano*
Salt	*1/4 teaspoon sage*
Pepper	*1/4 teaspoon parsley flakes (or fresh parsley)*
1/4 cup butter	*1/4 cup Cointreau*

Wipe duckling inside and out and sprinkle it with salt and pepper. Place on rack in roasting pan in preheated 450°F. oven for 15 minutes. Reduce heat and continue roasting for about 20 minutes to the pound or until cooked, but not overcooked.

To test if duck is sufficiently cooked, put a two-pronged kitchen fork completely through the thigh of the leg and lift the duck out of the roasting pan, holding it up and over the pan a bit. If the fat that runs from the duck is clear, it is ready to take from the oven. However, if the fat is cloudy and there are streaks of red running through it, it is still far from ready to eat.

When the duck is cooked, remove it from the oven and let stand at room temperature until sufficiently cool to handle.

Remove the breast of the duck on both sides, leaving the leg and second joint attached to the carcass. Cut meat from breast bone so that you have two large pieces of duck.

Heat the butter in a large skillet and add the breast, skin side down. Sprinkle with herbs. Cook until skin side is crispy brown. Turn, pour the Cointreau over it, let it bubble up, then lower heat and allow to cook 5 more minutes.

Place breast on warm serving platter or plates, pour the juices—the butter and Cointreau—over the surface and serve at once.

SERVES: 2.

Chicken Sweet and Sour

2 tablespoons dry sherry
1 tablespoon soy sauce
1 teaspoon salt
1 egg

3 tablespoons cornstarch
2 1 1/2- to 2-pound frying chickens, cut into serving pieces
Oil for deep frying

SAUCE

1 cup chicken stock
1/4 pound fresh mushrooms, thinly sliced
1/2 cup bamboo shoots, thinly sliced
1 clove garlic, minced

1 tablespoon cornstarch
1 tablespoon dry sherry
1 tablespoon brown sugar
2 teaspoons soy sauce
1 teaspoon monosodium glutamate
1 to 2 teaspoons water

GARNISH

Chopped green onions

Sesame seeds

Combine sherry, soy sauce, salt, egg and cornstarch. Blend with wire whisk until smooth. Pour over chicken pieces in nonmetal bowl. Let stand at room temperature for 30 minutes to 1 hour. Drain.

Fill a deep, heavy pan to 4 inches from rim with cooking oil. Heat to 350°F. on deep-fat thermometer (or until a small cube of soft white bread will brown in 35 seconds). Add chicken pieces a few at a time and fry to a deep golden brown. Place cooked pieces on paper toweling to drain. Keep warm in a 250°F. oven until all pieces are fried and sauce is made.

To make sauce, combine chicken stock or broth with mushrooms and bamboo shoots. Bring to boil, then lower heat and allow to simmer gently until mushrooms are tender—5 to 7 minutes. In small bowl, mix remaining ingredients until smooth. Add to hot mixture and stir until sauce thickens.

Place chicken on serving platter, pour sauce over surface, sprinkle with green onion and sesame seeds. Serve at once.

SERVES: 4.

Baked Chicken Crepes with Mornay Sauce

CREPES

3 tablespoons all-purpose flour
1 egg yolk
1 whole egg

1/4 teaspoon salt
1/2 teaspoon sugar
1 cup milk

FILLING AND MORNAY SAUCE

1/4 cup butter
1/4 cup all-purpose flour
2 cups milk
1/2 teaspoon salt

1 cup finely diced white meat of chicken
2 egg yolks
1/2 cup plus 2 tablespoons grated Parmesan or Swiss cheese

Combine flour, egg yolk, egg, salt and sugar. Beat with wire whisk until smooth. Add milk, blend well and strain through a fine sieve. *Alternate method:* Place all ingredients in electric blender; blend until smooth. Strain through fine sieve. Let batter stand for 1 hour before making crepes.

Heat a 5-inch crepe (or omelet) pan and grease lightly with butter. Pour in about 2 tablespoons of the batter. Rotate pan so batter spreads over bottom evenly. Cook over medium heat until the top side is dry and underneath is lightly browned; turn and lightly brown second side. Do not stack crepes while hot.

NOTE: Crepes may be made ahead of time. Stack cooled crepes with wax paper between each layer, wrap stack in foil. Refrigerate or freeze until ready to use. Reheat 2 to 3 minutes in a moderate oven just before filling crepes.

Filling and Mornay sauce: Melt butter in top of double boiler, add flour and blend over moderate heat. Place pan over simmering water and slowly add milk. Stir until smooth, add salt and cook, stirring often, until sauce thickens. Add one cup of this sauce to the chicken, blend and set aside.

To make Mornay sauce: Beat egg yolks until well blended. Quickly blend in about 2 tablespoons of the remaining hot cream sauce, then stir this mixture back into the hot cream sauce. Stir in the ½ cup of grated cheese. Stir over simmering water until cheese melts.

Place some of the chicken-cream sauce filling in the center of each crepe. Fold crepe in half and then in half again. This will give you a triangle with an open end to it. Place filled crepes in single layer in long baking dish or place in individual small baking dishes (2 or 3 filled crepes in each small dish). Cover completely with Mornay sauce. Sprinkle grated cheese over surface and bake under moderate broiler heat for 6 to 8 minutes or until lightly browned.

Serve at once.

SERVES: 4 to 6.

Peacock Capon Soufflé

3/4 *pound chicken meat, boned,*   1/8 *teaspoon white pepper*
     skinned and finely ground   *Butter*
2 *egg whites*   *Freshly cooked white rice*
3/4 *cup heavy cream*   *Supreme sauce*
1/4 *teaspoon salt*   *Bing cherries*

Place ground chicken meat and egg whites in large bowl and mix well. Add cream and mix until chicken absorbs all liquid. Season with salt and pepper.

Place chicken mixture in 4 5- to 6-ounce well-buttered soufflé dishes. Place them in a pan filled with water to ½ inch of rim. Bring water to boil, then reduce heat until it barely simmers. Cover entire pan and cook soufflé for 15 to 18 minutes or until firm to the finger touch.

To serve: Unmold each soufflé onto a bed of freshly cooked hot white rice. Cover with supreme sauce and garnish with 2 or 3 fresh Bing cherries on stems.

SERVES: 4.

Duckling with Turnips

1 5- *to 6-pound duckling*   2 *tablespoons butter*
Salt   8 *small white onions, peeled*
1 *tablespoon flour*   2 *cups peeled and diced white*
1 *cup chicken stock*   *turnips*
3/4 *cup dry white wine*   1 *teaspoon sugar*

Wipe duck inside and out. Truss legs and wings close to body and sprinkle with salt. Place on rack in roasting pan in a preheated 450°F. oven. Roast for 25 to 35 minutes or until golden brown.

Remove duck to warm platter and pour off all but about 2 tablespoons of the fat from the pan.

Place pan over moderate heat on top of stove, add flour and stir until lightly browned. Add stock and wine. Cook, stirring constantly, until sauce thickens.

Return duck to pan with sauce. Cover and return to 400°F. oven for 25 to 30 minutes.

Melt butter in saucepan. Add onions; cook, stirring, for about 3 minutes over moderate heat. Add turnips, sprinkle with sugar and stir until vegetables are lightly browned on all sides. Add to roasting pan with duck. Reduce oven temperature to 375°F. and cook covered for a final 30 to 40 minutes.

Remove duck, carve and place on serving plate with turnips and onions. Correct seasoning of sauce with salt, pour over duck and serve.

SERVES: 4.

Roast Wild Goose California

MARINADE

1/3 cup vinegar
1 1/2 cups white table wine
   (Sauterne, Hock or Chablis)
Juice of 2 lemons
Juice of 1 orange
1 small onion, sliced
1/8 teaspoon nutmeg
1 small bay leaf
Few celery leaves

Few sprigs of parsley

1 goose, 12 to 14 pounds
Salt
Pepper
1 large tart apple, peeled, cored
   and sliced
2 stalks celery, cut into
   2 1/2-inch pieces

Combine ingredients listed under marinade. Pour over goose in large nonmetal bowl. Let stand 3 to 4 hours, turning and basting goose frequently.

Remove goose from marinade (reserve marinade), rub cavity with salt and pepper, stuff with apples and celery. Truss legs and wings close to body. Place breast side down on rack in roasting pan. Sear for 20 minutes in preheated 450°F. oven. Turn goose breast side up, cover pan, lower heat to 350°F. and continue roasting for 1 to 1½ hours or until tender. Baste occasionally with the marinade and pan drippings.

The Waldorf chef suggests: Serve with garnish of cling peach filled with currant jelly, or cling-peach slices simmered in currant jelly and a little butter.

SERVES: 6 to 8.

Chestnut Stuffing

1/2 pound fresh chestnuts
1 small whole onion
1 stalk celery
1 bay leaf

3 medium onions, finely chopped
1/2 cup chicken or goose fat
3 tablespoons Cognac or sherry

1-pound loaf soft white bread, crust removed and torn into small crumbs
1/4 teaspoon thyme
1/2 teaspoon salt
1/8 teaspoon freshly ground black pepper

Cover chestnuts with boiling water and boil until shells and skin can be easily removed (about 20 minutes).

Place blanched and shelled chestnuts in saucepan with onion, celery, bay leaf and just enough water to cover. Cook over moderate heat until tender.

Sauté onion in chicken or goose fat in large saucepan until limp but not browned. Remove from heat. Add remaining ingredients and blend well. Cool before stuffing poultry.

MAKES: sufficient stuffing for a 10- to 12-pound turkey or two 3- to 5-pound roasting chickens.

Any leftover stuffing may be baked separately in a well greased soufflé dish or ovenproof casserole.

Canard à l'Orange

(Roast Duck)

1 4- to 5-pound duck
1 cup orange juice ⎫
1/4 cup port wine ⎬ *mixed*
1 teaspoon salt ⎭

1 whole seedless orange, thinly
sliced but not peeled

Rinse duck inside and out with clear water. Dry well with paper toweling. Truss wings and legs close to body and place on rack breast side up in roasting pan. Do not cover. Roast in preheated 350°F. oven for 35 minutes per pound, basting every 10 minutes with a mixture of the orange juice, port wine and salt.

Arrange the orange slices around the duck on rack last 10 minutes of cooking time.

Place duck on serving platter or carve and arrange on serving plates. Garnish with orange slices.

SERVES: 4.

Breast of Chicken Marco Polo

2 whole chicken breasts
2 2-ounce slices of imported foie
  gras (goose liver)
Salt
All-purpose flour
Browned butter (see below)

Egg wash—1 whole egg beaten
  with 1/4 cup water
1 cup fine dry bread crumbs
4 tablespoons butter
2 tablespoons peanut or corn oil

Cut a one-inch slit or pocket in the thick side of each breast and insert a slice of the foie gras. Sprinkle the breast with salt and dredge with flour. Dip breast first in the egg wash and then in the bread crumbs. Press crumbs firmly into breast to make them adhere.

Place on rack and refrigerate 10 to 15 minutes (longer if desired). Heat the butter and oil in a heavy skillet. Cook the breast over moderate heat until lightly browned on both sides, then place in a preheated 350°F. oven for 10 to 15 minutes. Pour browned butter over each breast and serve.

SERVES: 2.

BROWNED BUTTER

Melt 2–3 tablespoons butter in a heavy saucepan. Cook over very low heat until it is a deep hazelnut brown. Use at once.

Excellent accompaniments for breast of chicken Marco Polo are oven-browned potatoes, scalloped (canned) artichoke bottoms and asparagus tips.

Ballotine of Capon Breast

1/2 cup soft bread crumbs
1/2 cup milk
1 egg, lightly beaten
1/2 teaspoon salt

1/4 teaspoon pepper
Pinch of garlic powder
1 1/2 cups cooked rice
6 double breasts of capon, boned
1/2 cup butter, melted

Place bread crumbs in mixing bowl. Add milk and egg. Blend and set aside 15 to 20 minutes. Blend in salt, pepper, garlic powder and rice.

Cut a deep pocket in each capon breast and fill with the bread-rice mixture.

Place stuffed breasts in baking dish and brush each with melted butter. Bake in a preheated 375°F. oven, basting frequently with the melted butter.

SERVES: 6.

NOTE: Boned chicken legs may be prepared in the same manner.

Chicken Cacciatore

2 1 1/2-pound frying chickens, disjointed, boned and cut in small pieces
Salt
Pepper
Flour
1/2 cup olive oil
1 small green pepper, seeded and cut in julienne strips

1/2 pound mushrooms, sliced
2 tablespoons flour
2 cups chicken stock or broth
2 cups (canned) stewed tomatoes
2 cups (red) Burgundy wine
Pinch each of thyme, marjoram, oregano and basil
Salt ⎫
Pepper ⎭ *to taste*

Sprinkle chicken pieces with salt and pepper. Dust lightly with flour. Heat oil in a large, deep skillet. Add chicken and cook, stirring, until meat is white and skin is lightly browned. Remove and set aside.

Add green pepper and mushrooms to skillet; cook, stirring, until limp. Stir in flour; when blended, slowly add stock and blend well. Return chicken to skillet and add remaining ingredients. Reduce heat to very low and allow sauce to simmer very gently for 20 to 25 minutes. Stir frequently. Correct seasoning with salt and pepper. Serve over freshly cooked thin spaghetti.

SERVES: 6 to 8.

Meat

Empire Room

The world famous nightclub, The Empire Room, is located off the Park Avenue lobby of The Waldorf-Astoria. Miss Peggy Lee, Tony Bennett, Ella Fitzgerald, Jack Benny, Joel Grey and Liza Minnelli are some of the top name stars who have played this room.

The period decor from which the room's name is derived, is enhanced by predominating colors of apricot and silver. Three huge Maria Therese chandeliers dominate the room, which is surrounded with graceful marble arches at the windows. Silver leaf rope sconces placed on ceiling-high, silver-framed mirrors, complete the memorable decor.

An evening in The Empire Room is a night that New York memories are made from.

Filet of Beef Wellington

PASTRY

5 cups all-purpose flour
1 teaspoon salt
3/4 cup butter
4 1/2 pounds center-cut filet of
   beef, trimmed of all skin and
   sinew
Salt
Pepper
1/4 pound shallots, finely chopped
1/4 pound butter
3/4 cup shortening

1 egg, lightly beaten
1/2 cup ice water, approximately

1 pound fresh mushrooms, finely
   chopped
1/3 cup flour
1/4 pound pâté de foie gras
Salt
Pepper
Egg wash—1 egg yolk lightly
   beaten with 1 tablespoon water

Place flour, salt, butter and shortening in mixing bowl. Blend with pastry blender or with your fingers until mixture resembles coarse-ground cornmeal. Add egg and sufficient ice water to form a smooth dough. Roll into a ball and refrigerate until well chilled.

Rub the filet with salt and pepper. Place on rack in a roasting pan and roast in a preheated 370°F. oven for 18 minutes. Remove from oven and cool to room temperature.

Sauté the shallots in the butter over low heat until limp but not browned. Add mushrooms and cook, stirring frequently, over moderate heat for 10 to 12 minutes, or until mushrooms are quite soft. Stir in the flour and mix to a smooth paste. Remove from heat and cool to room temperature. Add the pâté de foie gras, blend well and season to taste with salt and pepper.

Roll out the chilled dough on a lightly floured board into a rectangle about ¼ inch thick. Spread it with half the pâté mixture. Place the filet in the center and spread remaining pâté mixture over surface. Draw the long sides of the pastry up to overlap over the top of the filet; seal with egg wash.

Trim each end of pastry, make envelope folds, bring up over ends of filet; seal with egg wash.

Transfer the pastry-wrapped meat to a baking sheet. Brush all over with egg wash. If desired, cut out decorative shapes from the leftover pastry. Arrange attractively on top and brush with remaining egg wash.

Bake in a preheated 350°F. oven for 25 to 30 minutes.

Serve hot with or without a separate sauce, or chill and serve cold.

SERVES: 6 to 8.

Cold Filet of Beef Waldorf

*1 5- to 6-pound filet of beef, center
    cut
1 large carrot, scraped
1 teaspoon salt
1/2 teaspoon pepper
1-ounce can imported foie gras
    (goose liver)*

*1/4 cup cold water
1 package (1 tablespoon)
    unflavored gelatin
1 3/4 cups fine port wine*

Have your butcher trim the filet. With a sharp knife, cut a fairly deep slit down the center and insert the carrot in this pocket.

Rub the surface of the meat with salt and pepper. Place in a roasting pan in a preheated 450°F. oven. Roast for 35 minutes, basting often.

Remove meat from oven and allow to cool for 30 minutes. Remove carrot and stuff the opening with the foie gras. Bring meat to room temperature, then refrigerate until well chilled.

Sprinkle gelatin over cold water in top of double boiler, let stand 2 minutes to soften, then stir over simmering water until completely dissolved. Remove from heat, add wine, stir to blend. Refrigerate until slightly thickened but still liquid.

Place chilled filet in a shallow pan. Spoon the wine gelatin over it thickly. Pour any remaining gelatin around meat. Refrigerate again at least 5 hours, or overnight.

Cut filet into ½-inch slices and arrange attractively on a long platter. Surround with excess gelatin, cut in small dice.

MAKES: 12 servings as an entree, 18 to 24 servings when presented as the meat platter for a cold buffet supper.

Meat-Filled Crepe Fritters

CREPES

6 tablespoons all-purpose flour
2 egg yolks
2 whole eggs
1/2 teaspoon salt

1 teaspoon sugar
2 cups milk
Melted butter for cooking crepes

FILLING

1/2 cup finely minced onion
2 tablespoons butter
1/2 cup finely minced mushrooms
3/4 cup finely minced cooked beef
1/4 cup finely minced cooked pork
1/2 teaspoon salt

1/4 teaspoon pepper
Dash Tabasco sauce
1/2 cup all-purpose flour
1 egg, lightly beaten
1 1/2 cups fine dry bread crumbs
Vegetable oil for frying

Crepes: Combine flour, egg yolks, whole eggs, salt and sugar in large mixing bowl. Blend, then beat with wire whisk until smooth. Add milk, mix well and strain through a fine sieve. Set batter aside one hour before making crepes.

Heat a 5-inch crepe pan until a drop of water flicked on its surface will evaporate immediately. Using a pastry brush grease pan lightly with melted butter. Pour in about 2 tablespoons of the batter. Quickly rotate pan so batter spreads over bottom evenly. Cook until underside is lightly browned. Turn and lightly brown second side. Remove from pan and set aside. Repeat until all batter has been used. Keep warm while making crepes or stack when cool with wax paper between each crepe. Wrap stack in foil and refrigerate or freeze. Reheat briefly in 300°F. oven just before preparing filling.

Filling: Sauté onions in butter until limp but not browned. Add mushrooms and cook, stirring, for 5 minutes. Add beef and pork, cook for 10 more minutes. Season with salt, pepper and Tabasco sauce.

Spread filling on each crepe. Roll up. Cut each rolled crepe in half, trim off round ends. Dip each in flour, then in beaten egg and finally in bread crumbs. Secure with cocktail picks.

Fill deep, heavy saucepan to 3 inches from rim with cooking oil, Heat to 375°F. on deep-fat thermometer (or until small cube of soft white bread will brown in 30 seconds). Add prepared crepe rolls a few at a time and fry for 3 minutes or until nicely browned. Drain on paper toweling and serving at once.

SERVES: 8–10 as hors d'oeuvres.

Steak Poivrade (Venison Steak)

4 8-ounce venison steaks　　　　*Freshly ground black pepper*
1 cup sweet vermouth　　　　　*2 tablespoons bland cooking oil*
1 tablespoon wine vinegar　　　*2 tablespoons butter*
Salt

If possible, buy steaks 3 or 4 days before you are going to use them. Refrigerate covered.

The night before they are to be served—or 12 to 24 hours before cooking—place them in a nonmetal bowl and cover with the vermouth and vinegar. When ready to cook, remove from marinade, pat dry with paper toweling. Season with salt and a generous amount of pepper.

Heat the oil in a heavy skillet, add the steaks, brown them quickly on both sides, then cook to desired rareness. Venison steak, as all steak, is best when rare or medium rare. When overcooked, it becomes tough and loses a great deal of flavor.

Remove the steak to a serving platter, pour off the oil from the pan, place back on the heat. Add the butter, cook until lightly browned, pour over steak and serve.

SERVES: 4.

Filet of Beef Flambé

8 4-ounce slices of filet of beef	2 tablespoons cooking oil
Salt	1 teaspoon flour
Pepper	3 tablespoons dry red wine
1 tablespoon butter	1 tablespoon Cognac or brandy

Place filet slices between pieces of wax paper and flatten slightly by pounding with a mallet or rolling pin. Sprinkle flattened slices with salt and pepper.

Heat the oil and butter in a skillet or, if preferred, a chafing dish. Add the filets and brown each piece on both sides.

Transfer meat to a warm platter and stir the flour into the cooking fat in the skillet. When lightly browned add the wine and blend to a smooth sauce.

Return the filet slices to the skillet and cook a half minute. Pour Cognac over surface and ignite.

Serve filet slices flaming. Ladle sauce over each portion.

SERVES: 4.

Breaded Veal Chops Milanese
with Fried Zucchini

4 8-ounce veal chops	1 cup fine dry bread crumbs
All-purpose flour	Oil for frying
Salt	Fried zucchini (see below)
Egg wash—of 2 eggs beaten with 1/4 cup water, 1 tablespoon olive oil	Milanese sauce (see below)

Have your butcher flatten the chops to ¼ inch thick. Dredge each chop with flour, sprinkle with salt, dip in egg wash, then in bread crumbs. Press crumbs into chops making sure every area of meat and bone is covered.

Fill a heavy ovenproof skillet to about ¼ inch with oil. Heat. Add chops and cook over medium heat until well browned on both sides.

Pour off oil from skillet and transfer chops to preheated 375°F. oven for 8 to 10 minutes.

Arrange chops on serving plate with fried zucchini. Serve with milanese sauce.

Prepare zucchini for frying while preparing chops. Fry after veal is placed in the oven.

FRIED ZUCCHINI

2 medium zucchini
All-purpose flour
Salt
Egg wash—of 1 egg with 2 table-
   spoons of water, 2 teaspoons
   olive oil

3/4 cup fine dry bread crumbs
Oil for frying

Peel zucchini, trim off ends and cut into 1-inch finger lengths—about ¼ inch thick. They should resemble potatoes prepared for French frying. Dredge each piece with flour, sprinkle with salt, dip in egg wash and roll in bread crumbs.

Fill a heavy skillet to about ¼ inch with oil. Heat. Add the zucchini fingers and fry a few at a time until lightly browned on all sides—only about 3 to 4 minutes. Zucchini is best when not over-cooked. Drain on paper toweling. Serve with veal chops.

MILANESE SAUCE

4–6 large fresh mushrooms, thinly
   sliced
2 tablespoons butter
1 2-ounce slice boiled beef tongue,
   cut into narrow strips
1 2-ounce slice boiled or baked
   chicken, cut into thin strips

1 1/2 cups rich tomato sauce,
   canned or homemade
Salt ⎱
Pepper ⎰ to taste

Sauté mushrooms in butter in saucepan for five minutes. Add remaining ingredients. Season to taste with salt and pepper. Cook over low heat 15 to 20 minutes. Serve with veal chops and zucchini.

Beef Stew

1 cup diced salt pork
1 tablespoon cooking oil or fat
2 to 2 1/2 pounds beef—any good cut that would not normally be used for roast—cut into 1 1/2-inch cubes
1 tablespoon salt
1 teaspoon pepper
12 to 15 small whole onions
6 medium carrots, cut in 2-inch pieces
2 shallots, chopped

1 clove garlic, crushed
2 tablespoons flour
2 cups dry red wine
1 1/2 cups beef stock or water
1 bouquet garni—made of three sprigs parsley, 2 stalks celery, 1 bay leaf, tied together with string
1/4 teaspoon thyme
1/4 pound medium or small fresh mushrooms
2 tablespoons butter

Place salt pork in oil or fat in deep ovenproof saucepan. Cook stirring frequently over medium heat. When crisp, remove with slotted spoon, drain on paper towel and set aside.

Season meat with salt and pepper, brown on all sides in the bacon fat. Add onions and carrots; cook, stirring, until vegetables are lightly browned. Drain fat from pan and stir in the shallots, garlic and flour. Place saucepan in a preheated 400°F. oven until flour turns a deep golden color. Then return it to top of stove. Add wine, stock, bouquet garni and thyme. (Meat should be completely covered with liquid; if not, add a little more stock or water.) Bring to boil, lower heat, partially cover pan and allow to simmer slowly 2 to 2½ hours or until meat is tender. (Exact time depends on cut of meat used.)

Just before stew is ready to serve, sauté mushrooms in butter in separate saucepan for about 5 minutes or until just tender. Remove meat, carrots and onion with a slotted spoon to serving dish. Add the salt pork and mushrooms. Keep hot.

Remove bouquet garni and skim any fat from surface of sauce. Correct seasoning with salt and pepper if needed. Strain into a second saucepan, bring to boil and pour over meat and vegetables. Serve at once.

SERVES: 6 to 8.

NOTE: If the stew cooked slowly, the sauce should be of just the right consistency. If it is cooked too quickly, however, it is apt to be overthick. In this case, a little clear beef stock may be added after sauce is strained.

Grilled Salisbury Steak Belmont

1 1/2 pounds finely ground beef, lean chuck
1/4 cup grated onion
1/4 cup grated raw green pepper
1 clove garlic, minced
3 tablespoons finely chopped parsley

1/4 teaspoon paprika
1 teaspoon salt
1/2 teaspoon pepper
1/2 teaspoon powdered thyme
1/4 cup all-purpose flour, seasoned with 1/2 teaspoon salt, 1/4 teaspoon pepper
1 tablespoon olive oil

SAUCE

1/3 cup butter
3/4 cup tomato catsup
2 tablespoons lemon juice
2 teaspoons Worcestershire sauce
Dash of Tabasco sauce

1 teaspoon prepared mustard
Pinch of mace
Salt ⎱ to taste
Pepper ⎰
1/4 cup dry sherry

Combine ground beef, onion, green pepper, garlic and parsley. Season with paprika, salt, pepper and thyme. Blend well and shape into 12 small steaks, about ¾ inch thick. Sprinkle lightly with seasoned flour and brush with olive oil.

Place on broiler rack about 3 inches below flame and broil from 5 to 6 minutes on each side depending on degree of doneness desired.

While steaks are broiling, prepare sauce. Melt the butter in a saucepan with the catsup, lemon juice, Worcestershire sauce, Tabasco sauce, mustard and mace. Season to taste with salt and pepper. Blend well, then stir in the sherry, and bring almost to the boiling point.

Arrange the steaks on a hot platter or on hot plates, pour sauce over them and serve at once.

SERVES: 6; makes 12 small steaks, 2 for each serving.

Stuffed Veal Chops with Mushrooms

4 thick 9- to 10-ounce veal chops
1 pound fresh mushrooms, finely chopped
2 tablespoons butter
1/2 teaspoon salt
1/3 cup grated Parmesan cheese

1/4 teaspoon pepper
2 tablespoons cooking oil
1 tablespoon butter
1 cup rich tomato or marinara sauce, canned or homemade

Have your butcher insert his knife into the side of each veal chop, making a small pocket.

Cook the mushrooms in the butter for 5 minutes, stirring often. Season with salt and pepper. Remove from heat and cool.

Insert a generous tablespoon of the mushrooms in the pocket of each veal chop. Press edges of chop together to hold filling firmly. Heat the oil and butter in a heavy skillet, add the chop and brown on both sides. Remove from skillet, drain off excess cooking oil and place in single layer in shallow baking dish. Cover with sauce and sprinkle with grated cheese.

Bake in a preheated 350°F. oven 25 to 30 minutes. Serve at once.

SERVES: 4.

Sauerbraten

MARINADE

1/2 cup vinegar
1/2 cup water
1 medium onion, sliced
1 clove

1/2 teaspoon freshly ground black
  pepper
1 bay leaf

1 1/2-pound fillet of beef
2 tablespoons of beef fat
1 marrow bone
1/2 cup red wine

1 medium onion, diced
1 medium tomato, peeled and
  diced

1 tablespoon flour
1/2 teaspoon sugar
Salt to taste

1 teaspoon butter
1 tablespoon sour cream

Combine ingredients listed under marinade in saucepan. Bring to boil, lower heat and allow to simmer gently for about 10 minutes.

Place meat in nonmetal bowl. Pour hot marinade over meat. Cover bowl tightly. Refrigerate 2 to 3 days, turning the meat in the marinade every 12 hours.

Drain meat (reserve marinade); pat dry.

Heat the beef fat in a deep heavy skillet. Add meat and marrow bone. Sear over high heat until brown on all sides. Add the onions, tomato, ½ cup of the reserved marinade and the wine. Cover and allow to simmer over low heat for one hour or until meat is tender. Turn meat several times as it cooks. When done, discard bone and transfer to a heated platter. Stir the flour into liquid remaining in skillet; blend well.

Strain remaining marinade. Add to liquid in skillet. Cook, stirring, over moderate heat, to a thick sauce. Add remaining ingredients, season to taste with salt, strain, pour over meat and serve.

SERVES: 4.

...nked Chopped Steak, antipasto of Diced Cooked Vegetables in Shell, Oscar's Chocolate Marble Cake.

Quiche Lorraine, Ballontine of Chicken Leg, caviar on ice, Strawberry Mousse.

Strawberry Mousse, Lobster Flambé, Pâté de Foie Gras au Gelée

Southern Cross Salad with mayonnaise, Peach Tart, Peacock Capon Soufflé, Bombe Vesuvius.

Waldorf Salad, finger sandwiches.

Beef Wellington, nest of Pommes Beignets, stuffed artichokes, salad.

Bouillabaisse Marseillaise.

Roast Ribs of Beef, Yorkshire Pudding

*Steak Tartare, cold salmon glazed with wine aspic
and garnished with pimiento halves and hard-
cooked egg slices.*

Duck à l'Orange, Hilton Orange.

Hasenpfeffer (Rabbit Stew)

1 *young rabbit, about 2 to 2 1/2*
pounds

MARINADE

1 *onion, sliced*	1 *sprig parsley*
1 *carrot, scraped and sliced*	1/4 *teaspoon thyme*
1 *clove garlic*	1 *tablespoon salt*
1 *cup dry red wine*	6 *peppercorns*
1 *bay leaf*	2 *tablespoons olive oil*
1/2 *cup cooking oil*	1 *tablespoon flour*
1 *carrot, sliced*	1 1/2 *cups dry red wine*
1 *onion, chopped*	2 *cups clear chicken stock*
2 *shallots*	1/2 *teaspoon salt*
1 *clove garlic, chopped*	1/8 *teaspoon pepper*

Cut rabbit into serving pieces. Place in earthenware (or other nonmetal) bowl. Add ingredients listed under marinade. Cover bowl and keep in cool place for 24 to 48 hours. Turn meat in marinade every 8 hours.

Wipe marinated meat dry and sprinkle with salt and pepper. Reserve marinade.

Heat the oil in a deep, heavy skillet, one with flameproof handle. Add the rabbit pieces and cook over medium-high heat until golden brown. Add carrots and onions and cook a few seconds. Pour off almost all of the oil from the pan, add shallots and garlic. Stir in flour and blend well. Place skillet in a preheated 350°F. oven until flour is lightly browned. Return skillet to top of stove and add the wine, the reserved marinade and stock. Bring to boil and skim surface. Lower heat, partially cover skillet and simmer gently 1½ hours.

Transfer meat to a second pan. Allow gravy to stand at room temperature about 15 minutes. Remove fat from surface, strain gravy and add to the meat. Cook over low heat until rabbit is tender, about 30 minutes. Correct seasoning and serve.

SERVES: 4.

Beef Stew Flamande

2 tablespoons butter
2 tablespoons flour
2 cups beef stock
2 tablespoons tomato purée
2 cups beer
Salt   ⎫
Pepper ⎬ to taste

1 tablespoon oil or shortening
2 pounds top sirloin of beef, cut in
   1 1/2- by 1-inch cubes
1 large onion, chopped
1 clove garlic, minced

Melt butter in a large, heavy saucepan. Stir in flour and cook, stirring, until lightly browned. Slowly add stock, stirring it into the flour as it is added. Cook over low heat, stirring frequently, until sauce is smooth and thick. Remove from heat. Add tomato purée and beer. Season to taste with salt and pepper. Set aside.

Heat the oil or shortening in an ovenproof skillet. Add the meat and brown on all sides. Add onion and garlic. Cook, stirring, until onion is limp. Add the prepared sauce. Blend. Cover and transfer skillet to a preheated 350°F. oven for 1½ to 2 hours or until meat is very tender. Correct seasoning with salt and pepper.

Serve with boiled potatoes or rice.

SERVES: 4 to 6.

Beef Stroganoff

1 large onion, chopped
1 clove garlic
5 tablespoons butter
1 teaspoon crushed peppercorns
3/4 cup apple-cider vinegar
3 tablespoons flour
1 cup beef stock or broth

2 cups milk
1/4 cup sour cream
Salt to taste
2 tablespoons shortening
1 1/2 pounds beef tenderloin,
   cut in thin strips, 1 1/2 inch by
   1/4 inch

Sauté onion and garlic in 2 tablespoons of the butter until limp. Add peppercorns and vinegar. Cook over low heat until vinegar is reduced to about ⅓ cup. Remove from heat, strain and set aside.

Melt remaining butter in a large heavy saucepan. Add flour and stir until lightly browned. Slowly add stock, stirring it into the flour as it is added. Add milk and cook, stirring, over low heat to a thick, smooth sauce. Add strained vinegar blend and sour cream. Remove from heat and correct seasoning with salt.

Heat shortening in a heavy skillet, add meat strips and cook over high heat until browned (meat should be rare). Remove with slotted spoon, drain briefly and add to sauce.

Reheat sauce and meat but do not allow sauce to boil. Serve over white or wild rice.

SERVES: 4 to 6.

Grilled Filet Mignon Rossini with Pâté de Foie Gras

2 pounds center-cut filet of beef, cut in six uniform slices
2 tablespoons butter
1 tablespoon flour
1 1/2 cups beef stock
1/2 cup dry red wine

1 tablespoon puréed white truffles (may be purchased as such in gourmet food shops)
Salt
Freshly ground black pepper
6 small slices of pâté de foie gras

Bring beef slices to room temperature. Melt butter in saucepan, stir in flour and cook, stirring, over low heat until lightly browned. Slowly add stock, stirring it into the flour as it is added. Add wine and cook, stirring, until sauce thickens. Stir in puréed truffles and blend well. Season to taste with salt and pepper.

Place beef slices about 3 inches under preheated high broiler heat. Broil, turning once, to desired degree of rareness. Arrange on serving plates and place a slice of pâté de foie gras on each.

Reheat sauce if necessary and spoon over each serving.

SERVES: 6.

Zraziki po Krakowsku (Beef Roll-Ups, from Poland)

2 *pounds round steak cut*	1 *small onion, minced*
1/4 inch thick	1 *egg, slightly beaten*
2 *teaspoons salt*	*Flour*
2 *teaspoons pepper*	2 *cups meat stock or broth,*
1/2 cup butter	*canned or homemade*
2 *cups soft bread crumbs*	1 *tablespoon chopped parsley*

Cut round steak into strips about 4½ by 2 inches, sprinkle with half the salt and pepper. Pound each piece with a wooden mallet or the edge of a heavy plate to flatten slightly.

Melt ¼ cup of the butter and combine with bread crumbs, onion, egg, remaining salt and pepper. Spread mixture on pieces of meat, roll up and fasten with skewers or toothpicks.

Dredge meat rolls with flour and brown in the remaining ¼ cup of butter in a heavy skillet. Add stock, cover and simmer for about 2 hours, or until meat is tender. Remove skewers or toothpicks and place roll-ups on a heated platter. Pour gravy over surface; sprinkle with chopped parsley and serve.

SERVES: 5 to 6.

Steak Tartare

1 *pound lean top round of beef,*	*Egg yolk*
put through meat grinder twice	*Bread croustade (see below)*
1 *teaspoon minced onion*	*Anchovy filets*
1 *teaspoon minced parsley*	*Capers*
1 *teaspoon Worcestershire sauce*	*Lettuce*
1/4 teaspoon prepared mustard	*Parsley*
1/2 teaspoon salt	*Chopped onion*
1/4 teaspoon freshly ground black	*Thin slices of dill pickle*
pepper	

Combine beef, minced onion, parsley, Worcestershire sauce, mustard, salt and pepper. Blend well and form into loaf. Cover and refrigerate until well chilled. Place on serving plate. Place unbroken egg yolk in prepared croustade and place in center of meat. Top with anchovy filets. Garnish platter with lettuce leaves filled with capers and chopped onion. Place dill-pickle slices between each, alternately with mounds of coarsely chopped pickles.

SERVES: 4.

BREAD CROUSTADES

Cut crust from soft white-bread slices. Cut with biscuit cutter in rounds. Dip rounds in melted butter. Place in small muffin tins, pressing them down into the tins to form little "cups." Bake in a preheated 300°F. oven until lightly browned and crisp. Cool and use as needed.

Oscar's Planked Chopped Steak

2 pounds ground sirloin
1 tablespoon butter
1 tablespoon oil
Salt
Butter

Freshly ground black pepper
Duchess potatoes (see below)
6 very small boiled carrots
2 cups cooked green peas

Shape meat into four large oval patties. Heat butter and oil in a heavy skillet, add meat patties and cook over high heat until well browned on both sides.

Place each patty on a lightly greased individual wooden steak plank. Sprinkle surface with salt and pepper. Surround with duchess potatoes. Place planks about 4 inches under broiler heat and broil until potatoes are lightly browned.

While meat and potatoes broil, heat the boiled carrots and peas separately in small amounts of butter. Add to plank just before serving.

SERVES: 4.

DUCHESS POTATOES

1 1/2 pounds potatoes   *2 eggs, lightly beaten*
1 1/2 cups water   *Pepper and salt to taste*
2 tablespoons butter

Peel and cut potatoes into quarters. Place them in a saucepan with the water. Cover and cook until tender. Drain, then dry by shaking pan over heat. Place in mixing bowl with the butter and mash until very smooth. Add the beaten eggs and continue to beat until very light and fluffy. Season with pepper and salt to taste.

Duchess potatoes may be made ahead (brush with melted butter to keep crust from forming).

When ready to use, they may be piped through a pastry tube or placed by spoonfuls around any meat or fish dish.

Beef Steak Sauté

Most people feel that a steak should always be broiled. Not necessarily so. When you cook a steak in a very hot pan, you sear it immediately; in other words, you seal in the flavor and the juices of the steak.

This is exactly what you do when you cook a steak over open coals —one reason a steak cooked on the charcoal grill in the back yard is so good.

When you broil a steak in the broiler, there is a tendency of pushing the flavor and juices out of the meat onto the drip pan under the broiler.

Any particular beef steak desired, whether it be a sirloin or a filet mignon, can be cooked on top of the stove with little or no fat in the skillet. Simply sprinkle salt on a hot skillet and sauté the steak on both sides until desired doneness.

The proper accompaniments for steak cooked in this manner are French-fried onions, fried parsley and broiled tomatoes. The French-fried onions should be firm, peeled or skinned. Cut into slices about a quarter of an inch thick. Then push the slices through with your fingers so you have ringlets of onions. Submerge these ringlets into ⅓ light cream, ⅔ milk. Let soak in this mixture for ½ hour. Remove, salt slightly, and flour well. Shake excess flour off, and plunge into very hot cooking oil, about 4 inches deep. Browning shouldn't take any longer than 3 or 4 minutes.

Remove to a paper towel to absorb all excess grease. Keep warm in a moderate oven until steaks are done. In the same cooking oil that you have cooked the onions (keep pan hot) fry one small bunch of well-washed and well-drained parsley, put this into the hot fat for about 4½ minutes. Remove immediately onto a paper towel to remove excess grease.

Place steaks on a platter, arrange the fried onions on top of the steaks, sprinkle over the onions the fried parsley. Garnish the platter with broiled fresh tomato halves that have been sprinkled before broiling with ⅓ bread crumbs and ⅔ grated Parmesan cheese.

NOTE: Parsley will cause the hot oil to splatter if it is not thoroughly dried. Pat dry with paper toweling before frying.

Filet of Beef Flambé

8 4-ounce slices of filet of beef	2 tablespoons minced chives
Salt	1 teaspoon flour
Pepper	3 tablespoons dry red wine
2 tablespoons cooking oil	1 tablespoon Cognac or brandy
1 tablespoon butter	

Place filet slices between pieces of wax paper and flatten slightly by pounding with a mallet or rolling pin. Sprinkle flattened slices with salt and pepper.

Heat the oil and butter in a skillet or, if preferred, a chafing dish. Add the filets and brown each piece on both sides.

Transfer meat to a warm platter. Add chives to skillet, cook, stirring, for a half minute, then stir in the flour. When flour is lightly browned, add the wine and blend to a smooth sauce.

Return the filet slices to the skillet and cook a half minute. Pour Cognac over surface and ignite.

Serve filet slices flaming. Ladle sauce over each portion.

SERVES: 4.

Ragout of Tenderloin of Beef

1 medium onion, chopped
1 tablespoon butter
3 large fresh mushrooms, minced
2 tablespoons tomato purée
1/2 cup brown sauce, or canned beef gravy
Salt
Freshly ground pepper } to taste

Cooking oil or butter
1 pound filet of beef—the ends of the tenderloin, cut into 1/8-inch-thick slices
1/4 cup dry sherry wine
2 tablespoons chopped parsley

Sauté the onions in the butter over medium heat until deep golden in color. Add the mushrooms, tomato purée and beef gravy. Season to taste with salt and pepper. Blend and cook over low heat, stirring frequently, for 4 to 5 minutes. Remove from heat. Set aside.

Grease a heavy skillet generously with cooking oil or butter. Place over high heat for a few seconds. Then add beef slices and cook, turning once, for about 5 minutes. Don't overcook; they should be medium rare. Remove meat from skillet and place in a deep, heated serving dish. Pour off any fat from the skillet, add the sherry and parsley, bring to boil. Add the reserved sauce. Blend and cook only until thoroughly heated. Pour over meat and serve.

SERVES: 4.

Roast Beef with Yorkshire Pudding

1 3-rib standing rib roast, 5 1/2   *Salt*
   to 6 pounds   *Freshly ground black pepper*

Preheat oven to 450°F. Wipe roast with a damp cloth and rub surface with salt. Place fat side up in a roasting pan without a rack. Roast uncovered for 20 minutes, reduce heat and continue roasting 1 hour and 35 minutes or until meat thermometer registers 140 (for rare) to 150 (for medium rare).

Remove meat from oven when desired degree of rareness is achieved. Place on warm platter in warm place while baking Yorkshire pudding.

SERVES: 6 to 8.

NOTE: After reducing heat, allow 10 to 12 minutes per pound for rare meat, 15 to 16 minutes per pound for medium-rare meat.

YORKSHIRE PUDDING

1 1/2 cups flour   *2 eggs*
1/4 teaspoon salt   *1/3 cup hot beef drippings from*
1 1/2 cups milk   *roast*

While beef roasts, sift dry ingredients into mixing bowl. Slowly add milk and beat until smooth. Add eggs one at a time, beating with rotary beater after each addition. Cover batter with a cloth and refrigerate until ready to bake.

As soon as roast has been removed from oven, bring oven temperature to 350°F. and spoon hot drippings from roasting pan to oblong baking pan. Place baking pan in oven until sizzling hot. Beat the chilled batter a few times and pour into hot pan to about ½ inch. Bake 25 to 30 minutes. Cut in squares in pan. Serve hot with roast beef.

SERVES: 6 to 8.

Scallopini of Veal Avocado

12 small veal scallops
2 tablespoons all-purpose flour
4 tablespoons butter
Salt
Freshly ground black pepper

1 large firm but ripe avocado
1/4 cup sherry, Madeira or
  Marsala wine
1/4 cup brown sauce (or canned
  beef gravy)

Pound scallops until thin. Rub flour lightly into each piece of meat.

Heat 3 tablespoons of the butter in a heavy skillet. Add scallops and sauté over medium heat until golden brown on both sides. Season with salt and pepper.

Remove scallops to a heated serving platter or plates.

Cut avocado in half lengthwise, peel and remove seed. Cut halves lengthwise into thin slices.

Add to the skillet in which scallops were cooked the wine, brown sauce and remaining tablespoon of butter. Blend and add avocado slices. Cook over low heat 5 minutes. Place avocado slices over scallops. Pour sauce over both and serve at once.

SERVES: 6 to 8.

Medallions of Veal with Prosciutto

8 4-ounce slices of veal, from the
  filet of veal or from saddle of
  veal
Salt
Pepper

All-purpose flour
4 tablespoons butter
3 tablespoons cooking oil
8 thin slices of prosciutto ham
Juice from half a lemon

Place veal slices between pieces of wax paper and flatten them slightly with a mallet or rolling pin. They should not be as thin as the veal slices used for scallopini—rather about ¼ inch thick and the size of large medals, hence, medallions.

Season each medallion with salt and pepper. Dredge with flour.

Heat 2 tablespoons of the butter with the oil in a heavy ovenproof skillet, add the veal and brown each piece on both sides. Pour off about half the cooking fat and place the skillet in a preheated 350°F. oven for 10 minutes. This will assure that the veal will be completely cooked, as it should be, yet not overcooked, crispy or tough.

Remove from oven and arrange medallions alternately with prosciutto slices on an oval ovenproof platter. Place platter in 300°F. oven while preparing lemon butter.

Heat the remaining two tablespoons butter in a small saucepan, add the lemon juice and cook over low heat until lightly browned. Pour over veal and ham. Serve with platter.

SERVES: 4.

Deviled Roast-Beef Bones

Deviled roast-beef bones are prepared in this manner. When the roast rib of beef has been sliced and you have used your portions of meat, the remaining bones can be kept the next day or even put in the freezer. Then you take them out and cut the bones so that the piece of meat remains on each side of the bone; in other words, you cut close to the first bone, skip over the second bone and cut close to the third bone. That gives you a bone in the middle with a wide piece of meat on both sides of it. The usual portion for a woman would be one of these bones, for a man two of these particular cuts of the bone.

A few hours before you plan to cook the bones, take them from the refrigerator and bring to room temperature.

Mix together 1 cup prepared mustard and 1 tablespoon brown sugar. With a pastry brush, or your fingers, paint the entire surface of each piece of meat and bone with this mixture. Place on a rack over a roasting pan and sprinkle liberally with fine dry bread crumbs. Place in a preheated 450°F. oven for about 20 minutes or until golden brown.

Some of the roast-beef gravy that you might have prepared for your regular roast can be used with these bones by adding a tablespoon of prepared mustard to every cup of gravy that you have left and heating well. The bones should be served piping hot from the oven with this sauce and it should be permissible, after you have taken away most of the meat with your knife and fork, to pick up the bone to enjoy the succulent close-to-the-bone meat.

Sliced Kidney Sauté with Armagnac

1 pound veal kidney	*1 tablespoon cooking oil*
Salt	*1/4 cup Armagnac (substitute*
All-purpose flour	*Cognac or any good brandy, if*
2 tablespoons butter	*desired)*

Remove fat, membranes and cores from kidneys. Cut into thin slices, sprinkle with salt and dredge with flour.

Heat one tablespoon of the butter with the oil in a chafing dish (or, if preferred, in a skillet) until it splatters when sprinkled lightly with flour. Add the kidney slices and sauté only until lightly browned. Do not overcook or kidneys will become tough. Pour cooking oils from pan and add the remaining tablespoon butter. Let it brown, then add the Armagnac (or brandy) and bring to boil. Tilt the pan slightly so that the fire "jumps into the pan" and ignites the sauce. Serve flaming.

Plain boiled rice makes a perfect accompaniment.

SERVES: 2.

Gulyassuppe

1/4 pound bacon, diced
1 clove garlic, minced
2 medium onions, thinly sliced and broken into rings
1/4 teaspoon paprika
1 teaspoon vinegar
1 pound beef chuck, cut into small cubes
1 teaspoon salt

1/8 teaspoon marjoram
1 tablespoon caraway seeds
1 1/2 quarts water
2 tablespoons flour
1/2 pound potatoes, peeled and diced
2 tablespoons tomato purée
2 beef frankfurters, sliced

Cook the bacon in a deep, heavy saucepan until done but not overcrisp. Remove with slotted spoon to paper toweling. Set aside. Pour off all but about 2 tablespoons fat from the pan. Add the garlic and onions and cook, stirring, until limp but not browned. Add paprika and vinegar. Blend well and cook, stirring, a half minute. Add meat, salt, marjoram, caraway seeds and 2 cups of the water. Cover pan partially and cook over medium heat until meat is tender and liquid has reduced to a thick sauce (about 1½ hours). Stir in flour, blend well, then add remaining water, potatoes and tomato purée. Allow soup to simmer gently until potatoes are quite soft. Add reserved bacon and frankfurters. Ladle into deep bowls and serve.

SERVES: 6.

Shirred Eggs with Sweetbread Fritters

1 pound sweetbreads	1/2 teaspoon salt
1 pint boiling water	1 tablespoon lemon juice

BATTER

1/2 cup flour	1/2 cup flat beer
1/4 teaspoon salt	1 egg white
1 egg	
1 tablespoon butter, melted, at room temperature	

Oil for frying fritters	8 eggs
Butter	

Soak sweetbreads in cold water for about 15 minutes. Cook in boiling salted water with lemon juice for 20 minutes. Plunge into cold water. Remove and discard tubes and membranes. Refrigerate covered while preparing fritter batter.

NOTE: Sweetbreads may be prepared ahead to this point. Refrigerate, covered, until ready to use.

Batter: Sift flour with salt into mixing bowl. Beat the egg lightly with the melted butter and stir it into the flour. Add the beer and blend only until smooth. Set aside at room temperature for 1 hour. Beat egg white until stiff and gently fold into batter.

Cut sweetbreads into slices 1¼ inches thick and about the size of a quarter.

Fill a deep, heavy saucepan with cooking oil to about 3 inches below rim. Heat to 375°F. on deep-fat thermometer (or until small cube of soft white bread will brown in 30 seconds).

Dip sweetbread slices in batter and fry a few at a time completely submerged in the hot fat. Remove with perforated spoon and drain on paper toweling. Keep warm while preparing eggs.

Butter 4 individual baking dishes and break two eggs into each. Bake in preheated 350°F. oven until whites are opaque and firm. Serve with hot sweetbread fritters.

SERVES: 4.

NOTE: Sweetbread fritters are also excellent served with a rich tomato sauce, your own or one of the good canned sauces now available at most supermarkets.

Roast Baby Lamb

Baron of lamb—the hindquarters of a baby lamb including both legs and both loins
Salt
Pepper
1 large onion, chopped
1 large carrot, scraped and cut in 1-inch chunks
2 stalks of celery, cut in 1-inch pieces
1 1/2 cups dry white wine
2 tablespoons lemon juice

Rub the lamb with salt and pepper. Place in a roasting pan with the onion, carrot and celery. Roast in a preheated 400°F. oven for 15 minutes. Reduce heat to 350°F. and roast for 18 to 20 minutes per pound in all. Half an hour before the cooking time is over, pour off all but about 4 tablespoons of the fat.

Pour the wine and lemon juice over the meat and finish the roasting, basting the lamb several times.

Roast Saddle of Lamb

Most people usually think of roast lamb as leg or crown roast of lamb, but the saddle, or the loin, as it is sometimes called, is the most succulent part of the animal.

Ask your butcher to give you the whole saddle, weighing from 7½ to 9 pounds. Have the flank part removed and some of the excess fat. Leave on the bone about 1 inch of the underskirt. Have this tucked under the saddle, and have the saddle tied.

Before roasting the saddle of lamb, it should be rubbed slightly with a clove of garlic and well seasoned with salt and pepper. Place fat side down in the roasting pan. Put into a preheated 450°F. oven and brown on all sides.

When it is well-browned, reduce the temperature to about 400°F. and continue cooking for about 20 minutes to the pound.

You may also surround the lamb after it is about half cooked with small new potatoes, scraped baby carrots and small whole white onions to be browned and cooked with the saddle of lamb.

When the lamb is cooked, remove from the oven and let set for 10 minutes. It is never good to slice any roasted piece of meat immediately after it is removed from the oven. This tends to make all the juices and flavor run out the minute it is sliced, rather than settling into the meat.

The saddle of lamb may be sliced on the bone by slicing lengthwise to the bone, then turn your knife parallel to the bone and remove the slices.

Serve accompanied by the roasted vegetables plus a good tossed salad.

SERVES: 6 to 8.

NOTE: Lamb roasted at 20 minutes to the pound will be pink and juicy. If well-done meat is desired, roast 25 minutes to the pound.

Vegetables

Artichokes with Wine-Cheese Butter

1/4 pound butter
2 tablespoons dry red wine
2 tablespoons grated Parmesan
cheese

Paprika
6 medium artichokes, prepared according to directions for Caesar
salad

Cream butter until fluffy. Blend in wine and cheese. Chill until slightly firm. Shape into a log in waxed paper. Chill until firm. Sprinkle heavily with paprika. Slice off rounds and drop into center of hot artichokes.

SERVES: 6 to 8.

Stuffed Artichokes
(Princess Margaret Dinner)

6 artichokes
1 cup vinegar
1 cup olive oil

2 hard-cooked eggs
1/4 cup finely minced (canned)
mushrooms
1/4 cup finely minced celery
1/4 cup finely minced fennel
2 quarts water

1 bay leaf
1/4 cup salt

1/2 cup finely minced prosciutto
ham
1 cup mayonnaise
1 tablespoon lemon juice
1 tablespoon mild mustard
Salt
Freshly ground black pepper

Wash artichokes. With a sharp knife cut off the stems, leaving flat bottoms that will permit them to stand upright on serving plates.

Combine vinegar, oil, water, bay leaf and salt in large kettle. Bring to boil. Add the artichokes, lower heat and allow them to simmer gently for about 30 minutes or until the leaves can be easily plucked off and the bottoms are tender.

Place artichokes upside down on rack to drain until cool.

With kitchen shears or a sharp knife, cut off the top third of each artichoke. Place them downward on a solid surface and press the leaves open, then remove the 'choke (fuzzy center) with a sharp knife or spoon.

Place in plastic bag and refrigerate while preparing filling.

Chop fine the whites of the hard-cooked eggs and combine them with the mushrooms, celery, fennel and ham.

Mix the mayonnaise with the lemon juice and mustard and fold into the vegetables and ham. Season with salt and pepper.

Stuff artichokes with this mixture. Refrigerate covered for one hour or longer to allow flavors to mellow and blend.

Put the hard-cooked egg yolk through a ricer and sprinkle over the surface of each stuffed artichoke just before serving.

SERVES: 6.

Artichokes with Vinaigrette Sauce

4 artichokes prepared according to
   basic directions under artichoke
   Caesar salad (see page 184)
3/4 cup olive or salad oil

1/2 cup vinegar
2 tablespoons sweet-pickle relish
3/4 teaspoon sugar
1 teaspoon seasoned salt

Prepare and chill artichokes. Stir together oil, vinegar, pickle relish, sugar and salt; chill. Stir again just before using. Serve vinaigrette sauce with chilled artichokes.

SERVES: 4.

Avocado-Stuffed Artichokes

6 *large artichokes*
1 *tablespoon salt*
4 *tablespoons vinegar*
8 *quarts boiling water*

4 *tablespoons wine vinegar*
6 *tablespoons salad oil*
3 *tablespoons olive oil*
1 *teaspoon salt*
1/4 *teaspoon freshly ground black pepper*

1/4 *teaspoon dry mustard*
1/2 *teaspoon sugar*

2 *medium avocados*
2 *teaspoons lemon juice*
3/4 *cup mayonnaise*
12 *anchovy fillets (about 2 ounces) chopped and drained*
1 *tablespoon capers, drained*
1/2 *teaspoon salt*
1/4 *teaspoon crushed red pepper*

With a sharp knife, cut stems from artichokes, leaving flat bottoms that will allow them to stand upright on a plate. Remove tough outside leaves.

Add salt, vinegar and artichokes to boiling water. Cook 30 to 40 minutes or until leaves pull out easily and bottoms are tender. Place upside down on a rack to drain thoroughly. When cool, separate the middle leaves and remove the 'choke (thistle).

Combine vinegar, salad oil, olive oil, salt, pepper, mustard and sugar. Blend and spoon over artichokes in nonmetal bowl. Cover and refrigerate until chilled.

Cut avocados in half lengthwise, remove seed and skin. Mash with fork until smooth. Combine with lemon juice, mayonnaise, anchovy fillets, capers, salt and pepper.

Drain artichokes. Spoon avocado mixture into centers and serve.

SERVES: 6.

Choux de Bruxelles Veroniques
(Brussels Sprouts with Grapes and White Wine)

1 1/2 cups chicken stock
2 pounds (2 quarts) fresh
  Brussels sprouts
1 cup seedless white grapes

2 tablespoons butter or margarine
1/2 cup dry white wine
Dash white pepper

Bring stock to boil in a large saucepan or chafing dish. Add Brussels sprouts; cover and cook over low heat 10 to 15 minutes or until almost tender. Stir in grapes, butter, wine and pepper. Cook 5 to 7 minutes longer. Drain off liquid before serving. (This drained liquid is excellent for flavoring soups or sauces.)

SERVES: 6 to 8.

Cavoli di Brusselle Alla Monachino
(Italian Brussels Sprouts Monk's Style)

2 pounds (2 quarts) fresh
  Brussels sprouts
Salt
1/3 cup olive oil
2 cloves garlic, crushed
2 tablespoons finely chopped
  seedless raisins

1 tablespoon capers
1/2 cup pitted black olives, sliced
2 tablespoons pine nuts
1 can (2 ounces) anchovy fillets,
  drained and chopped

Cover and cook Brussels sprouts in 1 inch boiling salted water 10 to 15 minutes, until tender; drain. Heat oil in large skillet; add remaining ingredients and cook 5 minutes over low heat. Add Brussels sprouts and cook, stirring, 5 minutes.

SERVES: 6 to 8.

Brussels Sprouts with Herb Mayonnaise

2 pounds (2 quarts) fresh
Brussels sprouts

Salt
1 medium onion, thinly sliced

HERB MAYONNAISE

2 cups mayonnaise
2 tablespoons finely chopped
parsley
1 tablespoon chopped chives

1 teaspoon crushed tarragon
1 teaspoon crushed chervil
1 teaspoon dill weed
1/2 teaspoon lemon juice

Place Brussels sprouts with onion in 1 inch boiling salted water in saucepan. Cover and cook 10 to 15 minutes or until tender. Chill in liquid, then drain.

Mix together remaining ingredients for herb mayonnaise; chill 2 hours. Combine with chilled Brussels sprouts. Arrange on crisp lettuce leaves. Serve as salad.

SERVES: 6 to 8.

Brussels Sprouts with Hungarian Dipping Sauce

1 cup water
2 chicken bouillon cubes
1/4 cup Tokay or dry white wine
1 pound (1 quart) fresh Brussels
sprouts
2 tablespoons butter or margarine

2 tablespoons flour
1 teaspoon salt
1/2 teaspoon caraway seed
1/4 teaspoon cayenne pepper
1 1/4 cups milk
1 1/2 cups commercial sour cream

Heat water in saucepan, add bouillon cubes; stir until dissolved. Add wine and Brussels sprouts. Cover and cook 10 to 15 minutes, or until just tender. Drain and keep warm.

Melt butter or margarine in saucepan. Blend in flour and seasonings. Slowly add milk and cook, stirring, until sauce thickens. Add sour cream; stir until well heated—do not allow to boil. Serve warm with the Brussels sprouts.

SERVES: 6 to 8 as an appetizer.

Brussels Sprouts with Orange Hollandaise

2 pounds (2 quarts) fresh Brussels
  sprouts
6 whole cloves
1 1/2 teaspoons grated orange
  peel
1/8 teaspoon pepper

6 egg yolks
1/2 teaspoon salt
Dash pepper and nutmeg
Juice from one orange
Juice from 1/2 lemon
1 cup melted butter

Place Brussels sprouts with cloves, the ½ teaspoon of the orange peel and the pepper in 1 inch of boiling salted water in saucepan. Cover and cook 5 to 10 minutes or until just tender; drain and keep warm.

Combine yolks, remaining orange peel and seasonings in electric blender; blend 5 seconds. Blend in orange and lemon juice over low speed; then gradually add bubbling hot butter, blending until thick. Pour into top half of double boiler and heat over just simmering water, stirring occasionally. Pour over hot Brussels sprouts and serve.

SERVES: 6 to 8.

Brussels Sprout and Peanut Fry

1 pound (1 quart) fresh Brussels
  sprouts
2 eggs, slightly beaten
2 teaspoons milk
2 teaspoons dry sherry

1 tablespoon grated onion
1 teaspoon salt
1/4 cup fine dry bread crumbs
1/2 cup finely chopped salted
  peanuts
1/2 cup butter

Place Brussels sprouts in 1 inch of boiling salted water in saucepan. Cover and cook 10 to 15 minutes, or until just tender; drain.

In small bowl, blend eggs, milk, sherry, onion and salt. In shallow pan, mix bread crumbs with peanuts. Dip Brussels sprouts in egg mixture; roll in peanut mixture. Melt butter in heavy skillet, add

Brussels sprouts and fry, turning frequently, until golden brown on all sides. Spear with toothpicks and serve as hot appetizer.

SERVES: 6 to 8.

Baked Celery Chinese

3 cups coarsely chopped celery
1/2 cup boiling water
Milk
1 tablespoon butter

1 tablespoon flour
Salt
1/4 cup chopped almonds
1 9-ounce can chow mein noodles
Paprika, to taste

Place celery in saucepan. Add water and cook over moderate heat for 10 minutes. Drain liquid from celery into measuring cup and add sufficient milk to make 1 cup liquid.

Melt butter in second saucepan, stir in flour; when bubbly, slowly add celery-milk liquid. Cook, stirring, until sauce thickens. Season with salt to taste.

Place half of the cooked celery in a greased casserole. Sprinkle with half the almonds and half of the noodles. Add remaining celery, almonds and noodles. Pour sauce over surface. Sprinkle with paprika and bake in a preheated 370°F. oven for 20 minutes.

SERVES: 6.

Baked Celery Hearts

1 cup chicken stock or consommé
1 teaspoon cornstarch

1 #2 can celery hearts, drained
1/2 cup grated Parmesan cheese

Combine chicken stock with cornstarch in saucepan. Cook, stirring, over moderate heat until slightly thickened. Remove from heat.

Place celery hearts in shallow baking dish, pour the hot stock around them and sprinkle the grated cheese over surface. Bake in a preheated 350°F. oven for 20 to 25 minutes.

SERVES: 4.

Braised Celery

6 celery hearts
1 cup chicken or beef stock
1 small onion, thinly sliced
1/2 teaspoon salt

1/2 small carrot, thinly sliced
Small piece of beef suet (1/2 by 1/4 inch)

Cut off most of the leaves and remove the tough outer ribs of the celery. Cut each heart lengthwise into halves and wash thoroughly. Drain, place in saucepan with remaining ingredients.

Bring to boil on top of stove. Transfer celery and liquid to baking dish, place in preheated 375°F. oven and bake until celery is tender—1 to 1½ hours.

Remove celery from cooking liquid. Serve with veal and chicken gravy or with a thin white sauce preferably made with the liquid used in cooking the celery.

SERVES: 4.

Cucumbers Doria

3 large cucumbers
Salted water

2 tablespoons butter
1 tablespoon minced chives

Peel cucumbers, cut lengthwise into fours and scrape out seeds.

Fill a shallow skillet with water, add a sprinkling of salt and bring to boil. Add cucumber slices and lower heat and allow to simmer until tender (6 to 8 minutes). Drain.

Heat butter in second saucepan. Add cucumber slices and chives. Cook 2 to 3 minutes (only until reheated).

Serve as garnish for fish or any seafood.

Tomato Fritters

2 eggs, well beaten
1/4 cup water
1 tablespoon olive oil
4 large, firm (slightly unripe)
   beefsteak tomatoes
1/2 teaspoon salt

1/2 teaspoon pepper
1/3 to 1/2 cup flour
1 cup fine dry bread crumbs
Olive oil, or olive oil and butter,
   half and half—for frying

Combine eggs, water and olive oil; blend well. Cut tomatoes in thick slices and sprinkle with salt and pepper. Dip them first in flour, then in the prepared egg mixture and finally in bread crumbs.

Fill a heavy skillet to about ¼ inch with olive oil or combined olive oil and butter. Heat the oil (or oil and butter) and add tomato slices in single layer. Do not overcrowd pan. Brown them on one side, then, using a spatula, carefully turn each slice over and brown the other side. Do not overcook or slices will fall apart. Serve immediately.

Tomato fritters are a good accompaniment for fried eggs or with broiled or sautéed fish on a Sunday morning.

SERVES: 4 to 6.

Baked Olive-Stuffed Tomatoes

6 medium tomatoes
2 tablespoons butter
1 small onion, chopped
1/2 small green pepper, minced
1 tablespoon sugar

1 cup chopped ripe olives
3 tablespoons soft bread crumbs
1 teaspoon salt
1/4 teaspoon pepper

Wash and dry tomatoes. Cut off tops and scoop out pulp with a small spoon. Reserve pulp.

Melt butter in saucepan, add onions and green pepper. Cook over very low heat until vegetables are quite soft—about 15 minutes. Add reserved pulp and remaining ingredients, blend well and fill tomato shells with the mixture. Place in shallow pan and bake in preheated 375°F. oven for 25 minutes or until tomatoes are tender.

SERVES: 6.

Carrot Soufflé

6 medium carrots	1/4 teaspoon salt
1 cup milk	1/4 teaspoon pepper
1 small onion, sliced	Dash of paprika
1/2 small bay leaf	Dash of nutmeg
1 clove	3 tablespoons grated Parmesan
1/3 cup butter	cheese
2 tablespoons flour	3 egg whites
3 egg yolks, lightly beaten	

Scrape carrots and cut into ¾-inch slices. Boil in salted water until tender. Drain and place in a generously buttered 2-quart soufflé mold.

Scald the milk with the onion slices, bay leaf and clove. Strain.

Heat the butter in a large saucepan, add the flour and stir until blended. Slowly add the scalded milk; cook, stirring, over moderate heat until smooth and thickened. Remove from heat, cool slightly. Blend in egg yolks, salt, pepper, paprika, nutmeg and cheese.

Beat egg whites until stiff but not dry, fold into sauce mixture. Pour over the carrots and bake in a 350°F. oven for 35 to 40 minutes or until soufflé is well puffed and firm.

SERVES: 6 to 8.

Pommes Beignets

2 pounds medium to small potatoes

1 1/2 cups water

PÂTÉ À CHOU

1 cup warm water
1/2 pound butter, cut into small
  pieces
2 cups flour
8 eggs

1 teaspoon salt
1/4 teaspoon pepper
2 eggs, lightly beaten

Peel potatoes and place with water in saucepan. Cover and cook over medium heat while preparing chou dough.

Combine water and butter in saucepan and place over medium heat.

When mixture comes to a full boil, remove from heat and add flour all at once. Stir until blended, return pan to heat and stir rapidly with a heavy wooden spoon until mixture leaves the sides of the pan and no longer clings to the spoon.

Remove from heat and add the eight eggs, one at a time, beating well after each addition. At this point the pâté à chou is ready to be combined with the potatoes. It may be set aside until they are tender.

When potatoes are done, drain off the water, then shake them in the pan over low heat until they are thoroughly dry. Transfer to a large mixing bowl and mash until very smooth and light. Season with salt and pepper, stir in the 2 lightly beaten eggs, add the chou dough and blend well.

While dough is still warm, place in a pastry bag with a star tip. To make each beignet, press out 3 stars close together (so that they are touching) on a baking sheet lined with buttered (parchment) paper. Without adding more dough, run the tip of the pastry bag lightly down the center of the three stars to make a strip of dough about 1 inch long.

Bake the beignets in a preheated 350°F. oven until they are well puffed and lightly browned. Serve at once.

MAKES: 2 to 2½ dozen beignets.

Delmonico Potatoes

2 tablespoons butter
2 tablespoons flour
1 cup scalded milk
1/2 teaspoon salt
1/4 teaspoon pepper

4 cups sliced cold boiled potatoes
3 pimientos, coarsely chopped
1/2 cup grated Swiss or American
cheese
1/2 cup fine dry bread crumbs
1 tablespoon melted butter

Heat butter in saucepan. Stir in flour; when bubbly, slowly stir in milk. Season with salt and pepper. Cook, stirring, until sauce thickens. Remove from heat.

Place half the potatoes in a shallow baking dish. Sprinkle with half the pimiento and grated cheese. Cover with half the sauce. Repeat with remaining potatoes, pimiento, cheese and sauce.

Mix bread crumbs with melted butter and sprinkle over surface. Bake in preheated 350°F. oven for 20 minutes or until surface is lightly browned.

SERVES: 6.

Colcannon Potatoes

15 large green onions, sliced
lengthwise and cut into 2-inch
lengths
1 1/2 cups milk
1 teaspoon salt
1 3/4 pounds potatoes, peeled and
diced

1 quart water
3 tablespoons butter
Salt
Freshly ground black ⎱ to taste
pepper ⎰
Milk as needed
Melted butter

In small saucepan soak onions in milk with half the salt for 30 minutes.

Cook potatoes with remaining salt and water until tender. While potatoes cook, place onions and milk over low heat, add butter and simmer slowly until onions are very soft.

Drain potatoes, place in large bowl and begin mashing. Gradually add the buttered hot milk and onions, pounding onions into potatoes. Continue mashing and stirring until potatoes become fluffy and onions are entirely absorbed. (In Ireland they use a wooden masher or pestle, and call this "beetling.") Add salt and pepper to taste and spoon mashed potatoes onto individual plates.

Make a depression in each serving and fill with melted butter.

Colcannon potatoes are traditionally eaten with a spoon from the outside in, dipping each spoonful into the melted butter.

SERVES: 6

Minted Peas

1 10-ounce package frozen green peas
Small bunch fresh mint leaves, 4–5 sprigs

1/2 teaspoon sugar
1 tablespoon butter

Cook peas according to package directions. Drain. Keep warm.

Wash sprigs of mint well under cold running water, drain, pat dry with paper toweling and remove stems. Place leaves on chopping board, sprinkle with sugar and coarse-chop.

Add butter to peas. Cook, stirring gently with fork, only until butter is melted. Remove from heat; add chopped sugared mint leaves. Blend lightly and serve.

SERVES: 6

Salads and Salad Dressings

The Bull and Bear

The Bull and Bear Restaurant on the street floor of the Waldorf reflects the warmth and charm of the late nineteenth-century English pub, in its deep-toned woods, burnished metals and the soft glow of "gas lamps." Throughout the room are paintings of hunting scenes and actual hunting equipment, such as horns, trophies and stuffed game birds.

A far cry from the old days of the Waldorf's men's bar, which was for the exclusive use of gentlemen, the Bull and Bear now caters to both sexes at cocktail time, for dinner and for supper. It still is, however, reserved for men only at luncheon except during the summer, when ladies are invited throughout the day.

The restaurant is distinctly Victorian in flavor. In the bar area, the walls are decorated with wood carvings of pheasants, an old fowling piece, hunting prints, brass and copper hunting horns and a red-fox weathervane. The tub chairs are upholstered in red velvet and the banquettes in this area are covered with multicolored velvet. In the Captain's Corner, which is a small dining room for not more than 30 guests, an antique ticker-tape machine which was used in the old days on Wall Street is on display.

Southern Cross Salad
with Avocado and Hearts of Palm

1 *small head romaine lettuce*
3 *heads Belgian endive*
1 *small bunch watercress*
1 *large avocado*
Lemon juice
6 *cherry tomatoes*

4 *(canned) hearts of palm,*
  drained
1 *teaspoon chopped parsley*
French, Roquefort or Russian
  dressing

Tear romaine into bite-size pieces. Trim away a little of the ends of each head of endive. Cut into bite-size cubes. Trim the tough stems from the watercress. Rinse all greens under cold running water. Drain and pat dry with paper toweling.

Place romaine in salad bowl, make a shallow indentation in the center and place endive in indentation. Arrange parsley sprigs over the endive, creating a tricolor arrangement; first, the light green of the romaine, then the white endive, and finally the dark green of the watercress.

Peel avocado, slice lengthwise and remove seed. Scoop out small balls with a melon scoop. Sprinkle balls with lemon juice.

Arrange avocado balls and cherry tomatoes on romaine. Cut each heart of palm slantwise into four pieces. Place between sprigs of watercress.

Sprinkle chopped parsley over endive. Bring salad and your choice of dressing to the table separately.

Blend and toss salad just before serving.

SERVES: 6 TO 8.

Pilgrim Fathers' Salad
(For Thanksgiving or During the Fall Season)

1 *head romaine lettuce*
2 *small heads Boston lettuce*
4 *heads Belgian endive*
1 *small bunch watercress*

1 *cup diced cooked beets*
1/2 *cup cooked kernel corn*
2 *chopped hard-cooked eggs*

DRESSING

1/2 *cup red-wine vinegar*
1 *tablespoon dry mustard*
1 *teaspoon salt*
1/2 *teaspoon freshly ground black pepper*

1 *tablespoon finely chopped fresh tarragon*
1 *tablespoon chopped chives*
1 *cup peanut oil*
1/2 *cup olive oil*

Tear romaine and Boston lettuce into bite-size pieces. Cut endive into 2-inch cubes. Wash all greens thoroughly, drain and pat on paper toweling. Combine greens in salad bowl, toss to blend. Remove tough stems from the watercress and place in the center of the bowl. Arrange beets, corn and chopped eggs around watercress. Refrigerate covered with plastic wrap while preparing dressing.

Combine vinegar, mustard, salt, pepper, tarragon and chives. Add peanut and olive oils. Blend well.

Bring salad and dressing to the table separately. Mix just before serving. The dressing should not be refrigerated.

When mixing a salad there is an expression of making the salad tired, in other words, working the greens and the garnish well with the dressing. The more you mix the salad, the more each leaf of lettuce is coated with the flavor of the dressing.

At the Waldorf, Pilgrim Fathers' Salad is sometimes served on a large platter and decorated with fall leaves.

SERVES: 6 to 8.

Seafood Salad of Halibut,
Shrimp and Crabmeat

1 cup dry white wine
1 cup water
Juice of half a lemon
2 teaspoons salt
1 pound halibut steak

1 pound flaked fresh crabmeat,
  chilled
1 pound boiled shrimp, peeled,
  deveined and chilled

1/2 cup prepared mayonnaise
1/4 cup chili sauce, strained
1 teaspoon dry sherry
8–10 crisp large leaves Boston
  lettuce
2 hard-cooked eggs, quartered
1 medium tomato, cut in wedges
1 teaspoon capers, drained
1 tablespoon finely diced mixed
  green and red peppers

Combine wine, water, lemon and salt in a large skillet. Bring to boil, lower heat and simmer five minutes. Add halibut and poach in this "court-bouillon" for 8 to 10 minutes or until flesh flakes easily with a fork. Drain and cool. Remove skin and bones. Flake. Refrigerate covered until well chilled.

When ready to prepare salad, combine chilled flaked halibut, flaked crabmeat and boiled shrimp; add mayonnaise, chili sauce and sherry. Toss lightly with fork until blended. Mound the prepared seafood in a large salad bowl lined with the lettuce leaves. Place quartered hard-cooked egg and tomato wedges around edge of bowl. Sprinkle capers and diced green and red peppers over seafood. Serve well chilled.

This salad may be served as a main course, a summer luncheon, a fish course or as an appetizer for a formal dinner.

To prepare for appetizer, mound salad on large slices of chilled tomatoes, top with slices of hard-cooked egg and garnish with parsley sprigs.

SERVES: 12 as an appetizer or first course or 6 as a main course salad.

Avocado Dilled Shrimp Salad

1/2 cup salad oil
1/4 cup white-wine vinegar
1 teaspoon dill weed
1/4 teaspoon salt
1/4 teaspoon pepper

1/2 small clove garlic, minced
24 cooked shrimp, peeled and
  deveined
3 large avocados
Lemon juice

Combine salad oil, vinegar, dill weed, salt, pepper and garlic. Blend and pour over shrimp in nonmetal bowl. Cover and refrigerate at least 8 hours—preferably overnight.

Cut avocados lengthwise into halves, remove seeds and brush cavities with lemon juice.

Arrange 4 shrimp in each avocado half. Drizzle with a little of the shrimp marinade and serve.

SERVES: 6.

Artichoke Caesar Salad

6 artichokes
3 teaspoons salt
1/2 cup olive or salad oil
1/4 cup lemon juice
2 cloves garlic, crushed
1 teaspoon dry mustard
1/2 teaspoon salt
1/4 teaspoon pepper

1 clove garlic, halved
5 cups torn romaine lettuce
4 cups torn Western iceberg
  lettuce
1 egg, lightly beaten
1 cup croutons
1/2 cup grated Parmesan cheese

Wash artichokes and cut in half, break off the tough leaves around the base and remove 'chokes (thistle part). Place artichoke halves in 1 inch boiling water and add ½ teaspoon salt for each artichoke. Cover and boil gently 20 to 45 minutes or until stems can be pierced easily with fork (add a little more boiling water if needed). Drain.

While artichokes are cooking, combine oil, lemon juice, crushed garlic and seasonings; pour into shallow bowl. Place artichoke halves in dressing; chill several hours. Rub salad bowl with garlic halves. Remove artichoke from dressing; arrange 2 halves on each salad plate. Combine dressing with lettuce in salad bowl, toss lightly, add egg and toss until greens are well coated. Mix in croutons and cheese. Heap salad between artichoke halves.

SERVES: 6.

Health Salad

2 cups shredded escarole
2 cups shredded carrots
2 cups cottage cheese
1 whole tomato, peeled, seeded and quartered

Fresh herbs (thyme, tarragon, dill, etc.)
Chives
1/2 cup French dressing

Line salad bowl with escarole; arrange alternating mounds of carrots and cottage cheese on top. Garnish with quartered tomatoes, herbs and chives. Serve with French dressing.

SERVES: 4.

Florida Salad

1 head Boston lettuce
2 large oranges, peeled, seeded and sectioned
2 cups grapefruit sections, fresh, frozen or canned

1 large avocado, peeled, seeded and sliced
1 small package cream cheese
1/2 cup lemon-cream dressing

Line salad bowl with lettuce, orange and grapefruit sections in a pinwheel design alternating with avocado slices. Roll cream cheese into small balls and use as garnish. Pour dressing over salad before serving.

All greens should be washed and then dried on paper toweling, and can be stored in a plastic bag in the refrigerator or used at once.

SERVES: 4.

Jersey Salad

1 head romaine
1/2 head escarole
1 cucumber, peeled and sliced
1 green pepper, cut in strips

4 green onions, cut in strips
4 radishes, sliced thin
4 ripe olives, finely chopped
1/2 cup French dressing
1/4 cup catsup

Combine first six ingredients in salad bowl; sprinkle with ripe olives. Combine French dressing and catsup, and pour over salad just before serving.

SERVES: 4.

Dakota Salad

1 head Boston lettuce
1 cup cole slaw
1/2 cup shredded raw carrots

1 cucumber, peeled and sliced
Fresh herbs (dill, thyme, tarragon, etc.)
1/2 cup sour-cream dressing

Combine first four ingredients, sprinkle with herbs. Toss with sour-cream dressing.

SERVES: 4.

New Mexico Salad

1/2 head Boston lettuce
2 bananas, peeled and sliced
2 tablespoons lemon juice
2 oranges, peeled, seeded and sectioned

1 avocado pear, peeled, seeded and sliced
1/2 cup lemon-cream dressing

Line salad bowl with lettuce. Sprinkle banana slices with lemon juice; arrange alternately with orange sections and avocado slices on lettuce. Pour lemon-cream dressing over salad just before serving.

Richmond Salad

1/2 head romaine
1/2 head escarole
1/2 head Boston lettuce
1/2 cup cooked string beans
1/2 cup cooked beets (sliced thin)

1/2 cup cooked diced chicken
3 green onions, sliced into strips
Fresh herbs
1 hard-cooked egg, cut in quarters
1/2 cup French dressing

Combine greens. Arrange string beans, beets and chicken alternately on top of lettuce; garnish with herbs and quarters of egg. Pour French dressing over salad just before serving.

SERVES: 4.

Arizona Salad

1 head Boston lettuce
1/2 head romaine, finely minced
2 boiled potatoes, peeled and sliced
1/2 cup boiled ham, cut in slivers

3 green onions, finely chopped
1 tomato, peeled, seeded and cut in quarters
1 hard-cooked egg, cut in quarters
1 tablespoon lemon juice
1/2 cup mayonnaise

Line salad bowl with Boston lettuce. Combine romaine, potatoes, ham and onions; pile on lettuce. Garnish with tomato and egg quarters. Combine lemon juice and mayonnaise and pour over salad before serving.

SERVES: 4.

Oregon Salad

1 head Boston lettuce
1/2 head escarole, minced
4 pear halves, fresh or canned
4 plums, seeded and cut in half

1 cup seedless grapes
1/2 green pepper, seeded and cut in julienne strips
1/2 cup lemon-cream dressing

Tear lettuce into bite-size pieces, place in salad bowl, sprinkle with minced escarole. Arrange fruit on greens; garnish with green pepper. Pour dressing over salad before serving.

SERVES: 4.

Carolina Salad

1 head romaine lettuce	2 tomatoes, peeled, seeded and
1 #2 can green asparagus	quartered
1 cup grapefruit sections (frozen,	1/2 green pepper, chopped
fresh or canned)	1/2 cup French dressing

Discard outer leaves of romaine, tear heart of lettuce into bite-size pieces and place in salad bowl; arrange asparagus, grapefruit sections and tomatoes on greens. Sprinkle with green pepper. Pour French dressing over salad before serving.

SERVES: 4.

Maryland Salad

1 head Boston lettuce	1 green pepper, seeded and cut in
1 cup lump crabmeat	julienne strips
8 shrimp (split)	2 tablespoons chives
1 tomato, peeled, seeded and	1/2 cup Thousand Island dressing
quartered	

Tear lettuce into bite-size pieces and place in salad bowl, pile crabmeat in center and arrange shrimp and tomato quarters alternately around crabmeat. Garnish with green pepper strips and chives. Pour dressing over salad before serving.

SERVES: 4.

Sacramento Salad

1/2 *head romaine lettuce*
1/2 *head escarole*
2 *slices of pineapple (cut in*
quarters)

2 *pear halves, fresh or canned,*
cut in quarters
1/2 *cup French dressing*

Tear romaine lettuce into bite-size pieces. Cut escarole into julienne strips. Combine in salad bowl; garnish with pineapple and pear quarters. Pour dressing over salad before serving.

SERVES: 4.

Chef's Salad

1/2 *head romaine lettuce*
1/2 *head escarole*
3 *stalks celery*
4 *radishes*
1 *large cucumber*
1 *green pepper*
1/2 *cup cooked ham, cut in*
julienne strips

1/2 *cup cooked tongue, cut in*
julienne strips
1 *large tomato, peeled, seeded and*
quartered
1 *tablespoon chives*
1/2 *cup French dressing*

Tear romaine into bite-size pieces; mince escarole and celery; cut radishes into thin slices; peel and dice cucumber; seed and slice green pepper into julienne strips. Combine in salad bowl. In the center, arrange a mound of the ham and tongue. Garnish with tomato quarters and chives. Pour dressing over salad before serving.

SERVES: 4.

Waldorf Salad

1 *cup diced apple*
1 *cup diced celery*
1/4 *cup mayonnaise*

4 *lettuce leaves*
2 *tablespoons chopped walnuts or*
pecans

Mix apples, celery and mayonnaise; pile in lettuce leaf on individual salad plates. Garnish with nutmeats.

SERVES: 4.

Salmon Salad

2 cups canned salmon
1/4 cup celery, finely diced
1/2 teaspoon mustard
1/4 cup mayonnaise

4 lettuce leaves
1 hard-cooked egg
1 tomato, peeled, seeded and
  quartered

Combine salmon, celery, mustard and mayonnaise and blend well. Pile into lettuce leaves and garnish with quarters of hard-cooked egg and tomatoes.

SERVES: 4.

Seafood Salad

1/4 cup cooked scallops
1/4 cup boiled diced lobster meat
1/4 cup boiled shrimp
1/4 cup cooked crabmeat

1/2 cup mayonnaise
1 teaspoon mustard
1 cup shredded mixed greens
1 tablespoon minced herbs

Mix seafood; combine mayonnaise and mustard and blend with seafood. Place in equal portions over shredded greens on individual serving plates. Garnish with herbs.

SERVES: 4.

Beef or Chicken Salad

2 cups boiled beef or chicken, cut
  in strips
1/2 cup mayonnaise
1 teaspoon mustard
1/2 head Boston lettuce
2 boiled potatoes, cold

1 cup cold boiled string beans
1 cup cold boiled peas
1 tomato, peeled, seeded and
  quartered
1 tablespoon chopped chives
1 tablespoon chopped herbs

Mix meat with mayonnaise blended with mustard. Arrange on lettuce leaves and surround with slices of potatoes, bouquets of green beans and mounds of peas. Garnish with chives and herbs.

SERVES: 4.

Ham and Tongue Salad

1 cup cooked ham, cut in julienne
strips
1 cup cooked tongue, cut in
julienne strips
1 cup cold cooked carrots, diced

1 cup cold cooked string beans
1 tomato, peeled, seeded and
quartered
1/2 cup vinaigrette sauce
1/2 head Boston lettuce

Mix meat and vegetables with vinaigrette sauce, serve on crisp
lettuce leaves.

SERVES: 4.

Chicken Salad

2 cups cold boiled white meat
chicken, diced
1 cup cold boiled dark meat, diced
1 cup diced celery
1/2 cup mayonnaise

1/2 teaspoon mustard
1/2 head Boston lettuce
1 tomato, peeled, seeded and
chopped
1 hard-cooked egg, quartered

Mix chicken with celery and mayonnaise blended with mustard.
Pile on lettuce leaves. Garnish with tomatoes and egg quarters.

SERVES: 4.

Gauloise Salad

1 head Boston lettuce
1/2 head escarole
1 cucumber, peeled and sliced
1 green pepper, seeded and cut in
julienne strips
1 pimiento, canned, cut in julienne
strips

4 green onions
4 radishes, sliced
6 ripe olives, chopped
2 tablespoons minced herbs
1/2 cup French dressing

Combine greens, cucumber and green pepper in salad bowl; garnish with pimiento, green onions and radishes. Sprinkle with olives
and herbs. Pour dressing over salad before serving.

SERVES: 4.

Anna Held Salad

1/2 *head romaine lettuce*
12 *orange sections, seeded*
12 *grapefruit sections, fresh or canned*

12 *blue grapes, peeled*
12 *walnuts*
1/2 *cup French dressing*

Arrange romaine leaves on individual plates. Place grapefruit and orange sections alternately on lettuce. Garnish with grapes and walnuts. Serve with French dressing.

SERVES: 4.

Belle Salad

1 *head endive*
4 *oranges, peeled, seeded and sectioned*

1 *cup strawberries, sliced*
4 *whole strawberries*
1/2 *cup French dressing*

Arrange endive leaves on individual plates, top with orange sections and sliced strawberries. Garnish with whole berry. Serve dressing separately.

SERVES: 4.

Adonis or Valentine Salad

1/2 *head Boston lettuce*
2 *tomatoes, peeled, cut in four thick slices*
1 *bunch watercress*
1 *4-ounce package cream cheese*

2 *tablespoons milk*
1 *cup cooked beets, chopped fine*
1 *green pepper, seeded and cut into heart shape with cookie cutter*
1/2 *cup French dressing*

Arrange lettuce leaves on individual salad plates, center with 1 thick slice tomato, surround with watercress. Mix cream cheese with milk and, using pastry decorator, pipe out a heart-shaped outline on tomato. Fill with chopped beets. Garnish with green pepper hearts. Serve dressing separately.

SERVES: 4.

Aiglon Salad

1/2 head Boston lettuce
2 tomatoes, peeled, seeded and
  quartered
1 cup cold cooked string beans
1 truffle, thinly sliced
1/2 cup mayonnaise

1 tablespoon lemon juice
1 tablespoon anchovy paste
1 tablespoon capers
1 tablespoon parsley, finely
  chopped

Arrange lettuce on individual salad plates. Blend tomatoes, string beans and truffles with mayonnaise which has been mixed with lemon juice and anchovy paste. Garnish with capers and parsley.

Salad à la Florentine

1/2 head Boston lettuce
1 cup celery, diced
2 cucumbers, peeled and diced

1 head endive, diced
1/2 cup mayonnaise
1 hard-cooked egg, chopped

Arrange lettuce on individual salad plates. Mix celery, cucumbers and endive with mayonnaise. Pile on lettuce and garnish with chopped egg.

SERVES: 4.

Chinese Salad

1/2 head Boston lettuce
2 mangoes, peeled and sliced

2 oranges, peeled, sectioned and
  seeded
1/2 cup French dressing

Place lettuce on individual serving plates; arrange mango slices and orange sections alternately on lettuce. Serve with French dressing.

SERVES: 4.

Green Goddess Dressing

1 clove garlic, minced
3 tablespoons finely chopped
  anchovies
3 tablespoons finely chopped
  chives
1 tablespoon lemon juice
3 tablespoons tarragon vinegar

1/2 cup heavy cream
1 cup mayonnaise
1/3 cup finely chopped parsley
Salt
Freshly ground black } to taste
  pepper

Combine ingredients in order listed. Blend well. Refrigerate until well chilled. Use as dressing for any green salad: romaine, chicory, and escarole perhaps, or combined head and leaf lettuce. Use a generous amount of dressing. Toss greens well and add additional salt and pepper as needed. Serve on individual plates or in small bowls to accompany a main course.

MAKES: about 2 cups.

Honey-Cream Dressing for Fruit Salad

1 cup mayonnaise
1/2 cup heavy cream, whipped
1/4 teaspoon salt

1 tablespoon lemon juice
2 tablespoons honey
1/4 teaspoon nutmeg

Combine mayonnaise with whipped cream. Fold in remaining ingredients. Refrigerate until well chilled.

MAKES: about 2 cups.

Cupid Dressing for Fruit Salad

1/2 pint fresh, carefully selected
  strawberries
2 tablespoons powdered sugar
1/4 cup Kirsch

1 cup prepared mayonnaise
1/4 cup imported Bar-Le-Duc
  currant jelly

Hull strawberries. Wash under cold running water and slice into a large mixing bowl, sprinkle with sugar, add Kirsch and blend lightly. Let marinate for 2 to 3 hours.

Combine mayonnaise and Bar-Le-Duc jelly. Blend and add to prepared strawberries.

This dressing or sauce is also excellent for ice-cream topping. It can be served as an old-fashioned strawberry shortcake by spooning it over hot baking-powder biscuit halves and topping with whipped cream. It can also be used for a filling for French pancakes or crepes— served warm.

MAKES: about 2½ cups.

French Dressing

5 whole eggs
1 clove garlic, crushed
1/4 teaspoon pepper
1 teaspoon salt

2 teaspoons paprika
3 cups of salad oil
1/2 cup red-wine vinegar
1/2 cup olive oil

Combine eggs, garlic, pepper, salt and paprika in large bowl. Beat with wire whisk until well blended. Add salad oil in slow, steady stream, beating constantly.

When mixture becomes quite thick, add half the vinegar. Continue beating, add olive oil and remaining vinegar and beat a half minute more.

MAKES: approximately 4 cups.

NOTE: This dressing may be kept indefinitely. Store covered in refrigerator. Use as needed.

Marinara Sauce

2 medium onions, chopped
1 clove garlic, minced
4 tablespoons olive oil
2 1/2 cups (canned) Italian
   tomatoes with basil
1/4 teaspoon oregano

2 anchovy fillets, chopped
1/4 teaspoon sugar
Salt
Freshly ground black } to taste
   pepper

In large saucepan, sauté onions and garlic in olive oil until limp but not browned (about 5 minutes). Add tomatoes and stir over high heat for five minutes. Turn heat very low and allow sauce to simmer gently for 30 minutes. Add anchovy fillets and sugar; season to taste with salt and pepper. Cook 10 minutes longer; add oregano. Serve over cooked pasta, chicken or seafood.

MAKES: 2 cups.

Horseradish-Cream Sauce

1/2 cup heavy cream
1/2 cup freshly grated horseradish
1 teaspoon vinegar
1/2 teaspoon prepared English
   mustard

Salt } to taste
Pepper }

Whip cream until stiff. Fold in the horseradish. Add remaining ingredients. Season to taste with salt and pepper. Blend well and serve at once. To accompany fish or meat.

MAKES: about 1½ cups.

Hollandaise Sauce

1/4 pound butter
4 egg yolks
2 tablespoons lemon juice or
  white-wine vinegar

Pinch of white pepper
Salt, to taste

Divide butter into 3 equal parts. Place egg yolks and one part of the butter in the top half of a double boiler. Place over hot but not boiling water over low heat. Stir rapidly and constantly with a wooden spoon until butter is melted. Add the second part of butter. Continue stirring until butter has melted and mixture thickens. Repeat with the final third of butter, stirring incessantly. Do not allow the water over which the sauce is cooking to come to a boil.

Remove from heat and continue beating for at least 2 minutes. Then stir in vinegar. Add a bit of pepper and season with salt. Replace the pan over the hot (but not boiling) water for 1 to 2 minutes, beating constantly. Remove from heat and serve at once.

MAKES: about 1½ cups.

Sauce Mousseline

Heat in a double boiler equal quantities of Hollandaise sauce and stiffly whipped cream, stirring very carefully and constantly until the sauce is thoroughly heated. Season to taste with salt and pepper and serve hot. For vegetables and fish.

MAKES: about 1½ cups.

Provençale Sauce for Chicken

2 tablespoons butter
1 onion, chopped
3 shallots, chopped
2 tablespoons flour
1/2 cup dry white wine
1 cup chicken stock or clear bouillon (canned or homemade)

2 medium tomatoes, peeled,
seeded and chopped (sub-
stitute 1/2 cup canned tomatoes if desired)
1 clove garlic, crushed
1/4 cup chopped cooked ham
1/2 teaspoon horseradish

Melt butter in a large saucepan. Add onions, sauté until limp but not brown. Add shallots and stir in flour. Cook, stirring, 1 to 2 minutes. Slowly add wine and stock and bring to boil, stirring until smooth. Add tomatoes and garlic. Reduce heat and allow sauce to simmer gently for about 30 minutes. Strain through a fine sieve set over a second sauce-pan. Press down hard on the vegetables with the back of a wooden spoon to force them through the sieve. Return to heat, add ham and horseradish. Correct seasoning with additional salt and pepper if needed and pour over hot baked, broiled or boiled chicken.

MAKES: about 2½ cups.

Entree and Dessert Sauces

Sherried Strawberry Sauce

2 cups frozen whole strawberries,
   thawed
1 medium orange, peeled and
   sliced
1/4 cup dry sherry

1/2 cup sugar
1 1/2 tablespoons grated orange
   peel
1 teaspoon ginger

Place half the strawberries and the orange in electric blender. Blend at high speed to a purée, or force strawberries and orange sections through a sieve. Combine with remaining ingredients. Refrigerate until well chilled. Serve over ice cream, cake squares, custard, frozen pie, etc.

MAKES: about 3 cups.

Sauce Grand Marnier

1 teaspoon vanilla
1 cup milk
4 egg yolks
3/4 cup sugar

1 cup heavy cream
1/8 teaspoon salt
1/2 cup Grand Marnier

Add vanilla to milk and scald. Beat egg yolks with sugar until light. Blend in cream, add salt. Gradually add scalded milk, beating with wire whisk until mixture is well blended. Transfer to top half of double boiler and cook, stirring, over barely simmering water until sauce is quite thick. Remove from heat and add the Grand Marnier. Refrigerate until well chilled. Serve with crepes soufflés.

MAKES: 4

Apricot Sauce

1 pound dried apricots   *1 tablespoon sugar*
2 cups water

Combine ingredients in saucepan. Cook over low heat, stirring often, until apricots are very tender. Remove from heat and strain through a fine sieve (or purée in blender). Refrigerate and serve chilled or reheat if desired and serve warm.

MAKES: about 4 cups.

Fruit Sauce from All Fruits

1 cup sugar   *2 tablespoons cold water*
1 cup fruit juice, any juice   *Whole or diced fresh or cooked*
1 cup water   *fruit (optional)*
1 teaspoon cornstarch

Combine sugar, fruit juice and water in saucepan. Place over medium heat and bring to boil. Lower heat and simmer gently for 10 minutes.

Mix cornstarch with water, blend and add to saucepan. Stir sauce until smooth and clear. Add fruit if desired. May be used hot or cold.

MAKES: about 3 cups.

Eggs and Breads

Oscar's

Oscar's, an unusual new coffeehouse, is located at the 50th Street and Lexington Avenue corner of the Waldorf-Astoria.

The new coffeehouse, with a New Orleans garden decor, has three separate areas for counter service, dining room, and cocktail lounge. Bright colors, treillage and open spaces create an atmosphere of light, warmth and cheerfulness.

Oscar's is open seven days a week for breakfast, lunch, tea, dinner, supper, cocktails, snacks—and sandwiches to go from Oscar's A-Go-Go. Oscar's opens every day at 7 A.M. and closes at midnight Mondays through Saturdays and at 10 P.M. on Sundays.

Date and Nut Bread

When cooled this bread can be thinly sliced. Spread with softened cream cheese or shredded cheddar blended half and half with butter. It makes a perfect accompaniment to a pot of hot tea.

2 cups boiling water
4 cups chopped, pitted dates
 (about 2 pounds)
3 tablespoons butter or margarine
3 eggs
2 cups sugar

5 cups flour, sifted
2 teaspoons soda
1/2 teaspoon salt
1 cup walnuts, chopped
1 teaspoon vanilla

Pour boiling water over dates and butter; stir and beat until the butter is melted and blended with the dates; cool. In a large bowl, beat together the eggs and sugar until light. Set aside 1 tablespoon flour; sift the rest of the flour with soda and salt into the sugar-egg mixture, alternately adding the date mixture. Stir until well blended. Mix the 1 tablespoon flour with the nuts and stir into batter along with the vanilla.

Turn into 2 greased loaf pans (about 9 by 5 by 3 inches each). Bake in a moderately slow oven (325°F.) for 1¼ hours, or until tester comes out clean. Cool 10 minutes, then turn out on a cake rack to cool.

MAKES: 2 loaves.

Rice Bread

1 cup unsifted rice flour
1/2 teaspoon salt
3 teaspoons baking powder
4 tablespoons vegetable shortening at room temperature

4 tablespoons sugar
2 egg yolks
1/2 cup milk
2 egg whites
1 ripe banana

Sift together rice flour, salt and baking powder. Cream shortening with sugar. Stir in egg yolks. Add flour alternately with milk, beating after each addition. Beat egg whites stiff, and fold (with rubber spatula) into mixture (do not beat in). Place banana in same bowl that held egg whites, beat banana to a smooth pulp and fold into batter. Spread in *well*-greased (with vegetable shortening) bread pan. Bake in preheated 325°F. oven about 45 minutes; bring heat to 450°F. last 5 minutes of baking.

Remove from oven and let stand 5 minutes before removing from pan.

Do not slice until cold.

MAKES: 1 loaf.

NOTE: Rice flour may be obtained at Japanese or Oriental food stores.

Olive-Cheese Muffins

A really great hot bread to accompany a luncheon salad. The cheese melts and bubbles up and over the muffins while baking—delicious!

1/2 cup pitted ripe olives	3/4 cup sifted all-purpose flour
1/2 cup soft or grated American cheese	1 tablespoon sugar
	2 teaspoons baking powder
2 tablespoons butter at room temperature	1/2 teaspoon salt
	1 egg
3/4 cup yellow cornmeal	1/2 cup milk
1/3 cup melted shortening	

Cut olives into medium-size pieces. Mix with cheese and butter. Sift dry ingredients into a bowl. Make a well in center. Add beaten egg, milk and shortening and stir only until dry ingredients are well dampened. Fill well-greased muffin pans with batter to about ⅔ full. Spoon a little cheese-olive mixture into top center of each muffin, pressing down lightly. Bake in 425°F. oven 20 to 25 minutes.

MAKES: 1 dozen large or 2 dozen small muffins.

Brioches

1 *package granular yeast*
1/4 *cup warm water*
4 1/2–5 *cups flour*
1/2 *cup butter at room*
  temperature
1/4 *cup sugar*

1/2 *teaspoon salt*
2 *cups milk, scalded and cooled*
6 *eggs*
Egg wash—of one egg beaten with
  2 tablespoons water

Dissolve yeast in warm water in large mixing bowl. Add 1 cup of the flour and mix to a smooth dough. Form dough into a smooth ball. Place in a well-buttered bowl. Cover and set aside until double in bulk.

Combine remaining flour, butter, sugar and salt. Add 2 eggs and half of the milk and mix to a dough. Knead until smooth and elastic. Add remaining milk and 2 eggs. Again mix and knead vigorously until very smooth. Combine with yeast sponge, add remaining 2 eggs and knead for 2 to 3 minutes. When perfectly smooth, place dough in a buttered bowl, cover and let rise in a warm place until double in bulk, 2 to 2½ hours.

Punch down and refrigerate, covered, 6 to 8 hours or overnight.

Shape dough into balls large enough to fill small brioche molds. Make a shallow incision in the top of each, place smaller balls of dough over the incisions and press firmly but gently in place.

Cover molds and let rise in a warm place until double in bulk.

Brush the surface of the brioche with egg wash. Place in preheated 375°F. oven and bake 20 to 25 minutes or until lightly browned.

MAKES: about 2 dozen small brioches.

Croissants

2 *envelopes granular yeast*
5 *cups flour, approximately*
3 *tablespoons sugar*
1/2 *teaspoon salt*
1/4 *cup warm butter*

2 *cups milk*
1 *egg, lightly beaten*
3/4 *pound butter, very cold*
Egg wash of 1 egg yolk blended
with 1 tablespoon milk

Soften yeast in water in large mixing bowl. Add one cup of flour and stir to a smooth dough. Cover bowl and set aside in a warm place until double in bulk.

Combine remaining flour, sugar and salt in a second large bowl. Add warm butter and milk and stir to a smooth dough. Stir in egg and combine with yeast dough. Cover and let rise for 15 to 20 minutes.

Cut cold butter into very thin slivers. Roll out dough to about ½ inch thick and distribute half of the butter slivers evenly over the surface. Fold ⅓ of the dough over the center and fold the remaining ⅓ over the top to make 3 layers. Roll out again to ½ inch thick and distribute remaining butter evenly over surface. Again roll out and fold over in 3 layers. Repeat folding and rolling twice again. Then fold a final time. Form into a ball and refrigerate until well chilled, about 1 hour.

Roll out chilled dough on lightly floured board to about ⅛ inch thick.

Cut into 5-inch squares. Cut squares diagonally making 2 triangles of each. Roll triangles starting from the longer side of the triangle and shape rolls into crescents. Place on a lightly floured baking sheet, cover and let rise in a warm place until double in bulk. Brush surfaces with egg wash. Place in preheated 400°F. oven for 5 minutes, reduce heat to 375°F. and bake for 15 to 20 minutes, or until lightly browned.

MAKES: about 3 dozen croissants.

Eggs Benedict

Hollandaise sauce (see below)
2 English muffins
Butter
4 slices of baked ham, cut in rounds
    to fit over English muffin halves

1 quart water
1 tablespoon vinegar
1 teaspoon salt
4 eggs

Prepare Hollandaise sauce (see below). Keep warm over hot water. Split and lightly toast English muffins, spread lightly with butter.

Sauté ham slices in butter only until thoroughly heated. Place one slice on each half English muffin. Keep muffin and ham warm in 250°F. oven while poaching eggs.

Bring water to boil in shallow pan. Add vinegar and salt. Lower heat so that water barely simmers. Break eggs, one at a time, into a saucer. Slip each gently into the simmering water. Cover pan and cook until eggs have set (about 5 minutes). Remove with skimmer (or slotted spatula), drain briefly and place over ham-covered muffins. Pour sauce over surface and serve at once.

SERVES: 4.

WALDORF HOLLANDAISE SAUCE

1/4 cup fine white wine vinegar
1/2 pound butter
3 egg yolks, lightly beaten

2 tablespoons water
Salt
White pepper

Place vinegar in the top half of a double boiler directly over very low heat until reduced to about ½ teaspoon. Remove saucepan from heat and set aside until vinegar is quite cool.

Place butter in top half of a second double boiler and place over hot, not boiling, water. When melted, gently pour it into a measuring cup, discarding the milky sediment in the bottom of the pan.

Beat the egg yolks and water in the double boiler with the vinegar. Place over barely simmering water and beat with a wire whisk until very light and frothy.

Slowly add the melted clarified butter, beating it into the eggs as it is added. Cook, beating constantly with whisk, until sauce is thick and smooth. Serve at once or keep warm over hot, but not boiling, water until ready to use (no more than 15 to 20 minutes).

NOTE: The trick to a perfect Hollandaise sauce is to beat constantly from the time that the eggs and water are put over heat until the final smooth, thick sauce is achieved.

Eggs Country Style

When eggs are cooked country style, they are cooked just as they come from the shell—no whipping or adding of cream or milk.

SCRAMBLED EGGS COUNTRY STYLE

Place a pat of butter in a skillet, heat skillet, then crack the eggs and gently place them in the skillet. When the whites are almost set, stir gently with a wooden spoon until eggs are cooked to your taste. Add salt, nothing else.

HAM AND EGGS OR BACON AND EGGS
COUNTRY STYLE

Place ham or bacon in skillet. When ham or bacon is almost cooked, pour off excess fat, add a pat of butter and place eggs gently on top of ham or bacon, and cook over low heat until done to taste.

Desserts

Sir Harry's Bar

The latest addition to the Waldorf-Astoria is the new Sir Harry's Bar, located in the Park Avenue lobby. The decor evokes the classic safari with stuffed animal heads, zebra skins and leopard upholstery in the room. Seated on the sofa are the authors of "The Waldorf-Astoria Cookbook," Ted James and Rosalind Cole. In the wicker chair is John Philip Cohane, author of "The Indestructible Irish."

Zabaglione

6 egg yolks
6 tablespoons granulated sugar
Few grains salt

6 tablespoons California sherry
wine

Combine egg yolks, sugar and salt in the upper part of a cold double boiler; beat with rotary beater until thick and lemon-colored; gradually beat in sherry wine. Place over hot (not boiling) water and beat with a rotary beater until thick and fluffy (about 4 to 6 minutes). Remove from heat and serve immediately in sherbet glasses.

SERVES: 4 to 6.

Omelet Norwegian
(Baked Alaska)

1 1-pound frozen pound cake (in
    foil loaf pan)
1 pint brick ice cream, any flavor

4 egg whites
1/2 cup sugar

Cut frozen pound cake lengthwise into 5 long thin slices. Place bottom slice on a flat heatproof cooking platter or any flat dish that can withstand high temperature.

Place ice cream on cake slice. Cover sides, top and ends of ice cream with remaining cake slices, trimming them to suit the shape of the ice cream. Cake should cover ice cream completely. (You will have bits and pieces of leftover cake. Reserve and use for another purpose.) Press cake firmly into ice cream and place in freezer for one hour or longer.

Preheat oven to 500°F.

Beat egg whites until stiff enough to form soft peaks, then gradually beat in sugar, beating after each addition. Beat to a smooth and shiny meringue.

Take cake-covered ice cream from freezer and cover entire surface as quickly as possible with a thick coating of the meringue. Place immediately in preheated oven. Bake for 3 to 4 minutes or until meringue is delicately browned.

Using a spatula, slip the omelet Norwegian quickly onto a chilled platter and serve at once.

SERVES: 6 to 8.

Basic Dessert Crepes

3/4 cup flour
1 tablespoon sugar
Pinch of salt
3 whole eggs
1 egg yolk
Melted butter for cooking crepes

1 3/4 cups milk
2 tablespoons melted butter, cooled
2 tablespoons Cognac or fine brandy

Sift flour with sugar and salt into mixing bowl. Beat whole eggs with egg yolk. Add to milk, blend and combine with dry ingredients. Beat with wire whisk to a smooth batter. Stir in melted butter and Cognac. Set batter aside at room temperature 1 to 2 hours before making crepes.

Heat a 5-inch crepe pan until a drop of water flecked on its surface will evaporate immediately. Using a pastry brush, grease the pan lightly with melted butter. Pour in about 2 tablespoons of batter and quickly rotate the pan so that the batter covers the bottom evenly. Cook until the underside is lightly browned. Turn and cook the second side until flecked with brown.

Remove from pan and set aside. Repeat until all batter has been used.

MAKES: about 20 crepes.

NOTE: Crepes may be made ahead and kept warm or reheated briefly in a 300°F. oven. Do not stack crepes while warm.

Crepes Suzette

3 tablespoons sugar
1/2 teaspoon grated orange rind
5 tablespoons sweet butter at room
  temperature
1/2 cup orange juice

1/2 teaspoon lemon juice
1/2 cup Grand Marnier, Cointreau
  or curaçao
1/4 cup Cognac or good brandy
20 dessert crepes (see page 214)

Traditionally, crepes Suzette are made in a chafing dish at the table.

Place sugar in a small bowl. Mix in the grated orange rind and 2 tablespoons of the butter. Set aside.

Combine remaining butter with the orange juice, lemon juice and Grand Marnier (or other liqueur). Stir over medium flame until butter melts. When it comes to a boil, stir in the sugar-butter mixture. Add the crepes to the sauce, spooning it over them liberally. Fold crepes in half, then in quarters, pour brandy over the surface and ignite. Serve flaming.

SERVES: 4.

Crepes Soufflés

3 1/2 tablespoons butter
1 1/2 tablespoons flour
1 cup milk
2–3 pinches of salt
1/2 cup sugar
1 teaspoon vanilla
4 egg yolks, well beaten

5 egg whites
20 dessert crepes (see page 214)
Confectioners' sugar
Cognac or brandy, warmed
Sauce Grand Marnier (see page
  201)

Melt butter in a saucepan. Add the flour and blend until smooth. Gradually add the milk, stirring constantly. Add salt, sugar and vanilla. Cook stirring over moderate heat until smooth and quite thick. Remove from heat, cool slightly, then quickly stir in well-beaten egg yolks.

215

Beat egg whites until stiff and fold them into the mixture. Set aside until cool.

Place a generous tablespoon of this filling just off the center of each crepe. Fold the crepe over it at the sides and ends, envelope fashion.

Arrange filled crepes in a single layer in a semi-deep baking dish. Place in a slightly larger pan filled with warm water extending as high as the crepes. Place in preheated 400°F. oven. Bake for 15 minutes, then reduce heat to 375°F. and continue baking 20 to 25 minutes or until crepes are well puffed.

Remove from oven, sprinkle surface with confectioners' sugar. Bring to table immediately. Pour on the warm Cognac, ignite and serve flaming.

Serve sauce Grand Marnier separately to spoon over each serving.

SERVES: 4.

NOTE: To warm Cognac, pour quantity to be used in a small pitcher, place in pan or bowl of hot water extending to depth of Cognac. Let stand 5 to 10 minutes.

Grapefruit Washington

2 grapefruits
1 8-ounce can fruit cocktail, well drained
2 tablespoons sugar
8 thin slices of pound cake

4 tablespoons rum
1 pint vanilla ice cream
2 egg whites
1/4 cup sugar

Cut grapefruits in half. Cut out sections and remove pulp from shell. Mix grapefruit section with fruit cocktail and the 2 tablespoons of sugar. Spoon this mixture back into grapefruit shells. Cover each with a slice of cake, sprinkle cake with rum, top with ice cream and cover ice cream with second slice of cake. Press cake, ice cream and fruit down into shells. Place in freezer. Preheat oven to 550°F.

Beat egg whites until stiff, then beat in the ¼ cup sugar. Remove prepared grapefruit halves from freezer, top with this meringue and place in preheated oven for 1 to 2 minutes or until meringue is lightly browned. Serve at once.

SERVES: 4.

Croquants

1/2 pound grated almonds
3 eggs, lightly beaten
1 cup brown sugar

1/2 cup flour
1/8 teaspoon salt
1 teaspoon vanilla

Combine all ingredients in large mixing bowl. Blend with your fingers to a stiff dough. Form into a ball, cover and refrigerate until well chilled.

Form chilled dough into small balls about the size of a walnut. Place on greased cookie sheet about 1½ inches apart. Flatten them with the bottom of a glass. Bake in preheated 375°F. oven until lightly browned, 10–12 minutes. Remove from pan with spatula while hot. Cool before storing.

MAKES: about 2 dozen cookies.

Cheese Cake

3/4 cup butter at room temperature
1 1/2 cups sugar
1 pound Farmers cheese
6 egg yolks
6 egg whites

3/4 cup flour
1 teaspoon cornstarch
1 1/2 cups heavy cream
1 teaspoon grated lemon rind
1 teaspoon vanilla

Cream butter with half of the sugar. Add Farmers cheese and continue creaming until mixture is smooth. Add egg yolks and blend well. Stir in flour and cornstarch. Add cream, lemon rind and vanilla. Blend to a smooth batter.

Beat egg whites until stiff enough to form soft peaks. Beat in sugar a little at a time, beating after each addition.

Fold beaten whites gently into batter; pour batter into a 9- by 3-inch well-greased cake pan. Place pan in larger pan of water with water extending to about 1½ inches of cake pan. Bake in preheated 385°F. oven for 1 hour and 20 minutes. Cool before removing from pan.

MAKES: one 9-inch cake.

Coupe Marie Louise *

* Ingredients for all coupes are for one serving. Simply multiply ingredients by the number to be served.

3 tablespoons crushed sweetened fresh strawberries

2 scoops strawberry ice cream
Whipped cream

Place one half the crushed strawberries in the bottom of a parfait glass, cover with ice cream, garnish with whipped cream and remainder of crushed berries.

Coupe Monte Carlo

2 tablespoons butterscotch or caramel sauce
2 scoops vanilla ice cream

1 gaufrette (French ice-cream wafer)
Whipped cream

Place the butterscotch sauce in the bottom of a parfait glass, top with ice cream, stick fan-shaped "gaufrette" into top, garnish with whipped cream.

Coupe Banana Fraisette

1 ripe banana (sliced)
2 scoops strawberry ice cream
Whipped cream

2 tablespoons Melba sauce
(bottled)

Arrange half of banana slices in the bottom of a shallow serving dish, cover with ice cream and remaining banana slices, top with Melba sauce and whipped cream.

Coupe Monte Cristo

2 tablespoons mixed canned fruit,
drained
2 scoops pistachio ice cream

1 tablespoon Melba sauce
(bottled)
Whipped cream

Arrange mixed fruit in bottom of shallow serving dish, cover with ice cream, top with Melba sauce and whipped cream.

Coupe Saint Augustine

4 dates (pitted)
2 scoops vanilla ice cream

2 tablespoons apricot jam
Whipped cream

Place dates in bottom of serving dish, cover with ice cream. Melt apricot jam over low heat until just liquid (about 3 minutes), pour over ice cream, garnish with whipped cream.

Coupe Jacques

1 *scoop lemon ice*
1 *scoop orange ice*
1 *orange section*

1 *grapefruit section*
Whipped cream

Combine orange and lemon ice in sherbet glass, top with oranges and grapefruit sections, garnish with whipped cream.

Coupe Cyrano

1 *tablespoon crushed pineapple*
1 *scoop vanilla ice cream*
1 *scoop raspberry ice*

1 *tablespoon Melba sauce*
  (bottled)
Whipped cream

Place crushed pineapple in bottom of parfait glass. Combine vanilla ice cream and raspberry ice, place over pineapple. Top with Melba sauce, garnish with whipped cream.

Coupe Ninon

1 *slice of pineapple (cut in half)*
1 *scoop vanilla ice cream*
1 *scoop orange ice*

1 *tablespoon apricot jam*
Whipped cream

Place pineapple slices on either side of shallow serving dish, add vanilla ice cream on one side, orange ice on the opposite. Melt apricot jam over low heat until just liquid, pour between ices. Garnish with whipped cream.

Banana Fernandez

1 *slice of banana (sliced length-*
wise)
2 *scoops of raspberry ice*

2 *tablespoons Melba sauce*
(bottled)
Whipped cream

Place banana slice in shallow oblong serving dish, add raspberry ice, top with Melba sauce, garnish with whipped cream.

Coupe à la Rock

2 *scoops of lemon ice*

1 *jigger of rum*

Place one scoop of lemon ice in bottom of parfait glass, make a hole on top with a coffee spoon, fill with rum, repeat with second scoop of ice.

Coupe Montmorency

5 *maraschino cherries*
1 *scoop vanilla ice cream*
1 *scoop raspberry ice*

2 *tablespoons Melba sauce*
(bottled)
Whipped cream

Place cherries on the bottom of a parfait glass, combine ice cream and ice, place over cherries, top with Melba sauce, garnish with whipped cream.

Coupe Maison

1 tablespoon chocolate sauce	3 ladyfingers
1 scoop vanilla ice cream	Whipped cream
1 scoop chocolate ice cream	Almonds, toasted and slivered

Place chocolate sauce in bottom of a parfait glass, combine vanilla and chocolate ice creams and add to glass. Stick ladyfingers into ice cream, garnish with whipped cream and sprinkle with almonds.

Coupe Alexandro

2 scoops strawberry ice cream	Whipped cream
1/2 fresh peach (sliced)	
2 tablespoons Melba sauce (bottled)	

Place ice cream in shallow serving dish, surround with peach slices, cover with Melba sauce and garnish with whipped cream.

Coupe Jubilee

5 black cherries (pitted)	Whipped cream
2 scoops vanilla ice cream	
2 tablespoons Melba sauce (bottled)	

Place cherries in bottom of parfait glass, top with ice cream, cover with Melba sauce and garnish with whipped cream.

Coupe Roosevelt

1 scoop vanilla ice cream
1 scoop strawberry ice cream
1/4 cup mixed fruit (fresh or canned), finely chopped

Whipped cream

Combine ice cream and place in parfait glass. Pour mixed fruit over ice cream and garnish with whipped cream.

Coupe Antigny

2 scoops strawberry ice cream
2 apricots, stoned and sliced

2 tablespoons Melba sauce
Whipped cream

Place ice cream in shallow serving dish, surround with apricot slices. Cover with Melba sauce and garnish with whipped cream.

Coupe Marie Antoinette

2 scoops vanilla ice cream
2 tablespoons strawberry jam
1 macaroon

3 black cherries (pitted)
Whipped cream

Place ice cream in shallow serving dish, melt strawberry jam over low heat until just melted, pour over ice cream, top with macaroon, garnish with cherries and whipped cream.

Coupe Mary Garden

2 scoops vanilla ice cream   Whipped cream
1/2 pear (canned or fresh), sliced
2 tablespoons Melba sauce
  (bottled)

Place ice cream in shallow serving dish, arrange pear slices around ice cream, top with Melba sauce, garnish with whipped cream.

Coupe Hawaiian

2 scoops lemon ice   Whipped cream
2 tablespoons crushed pineapple

Place lemon ice in shallow serving dish, top with crushed pineapple, garnish with whipped cream.

Coupe Florida

1 scoop lemon ice   2 tablespoons Melba sauce
1 scoop orange ice   (bottled)
2 orange sections   Whipped cream

Place ices in shallow serving dish, add orange sections, top with Melba sauce, garnish with whipped cream.

Coupe Belle Hélène

1/2 pear (canned), sliced
2 scoops vanilla ice cream

2 tablespoons chocolate sauce
Whipped cream

Place pear slices in shallow serving dish, top with ice cream, cover with chocolate sauce, garnish with whipped cream.

Coupe Louise

5 black cherries (pitted)
1 scoop vanilla ice cream
1 scoop chocolate ice cream

2 tablespoons Melba sauce
  (bottled)
Whipped cream

Place cherries in bottom of parfait glass, combine ice creams and add to glass. Top with Melba sauce, garnish with whipped cream.

Coupe Africaine

2 scoops of coffee ice cream
4 dates (pitted)

2 tablespoons chocolate sauce
Whipped cream

Place ice cream in shallow serving dish, surround with dates, cover with chocolate sauce, garnish with whipped cream.

Coupe aux Marrons

5 candied chestnuts (chopped)
2 scoops vanilla ice cream
1 jigger of rum

Whipped cream
1 whole candied chestnut

Place chopped chestnuts in bottom of parfait glass, add ice cream, cover with rum. Garnish with whipped cream and top with candied chestnut.

Coupe Empire

2 tablespoons Melba sauce (bottled)
1 scoop vanilla ice cream

1 scoop strawberry ice cream
1 tablespoon chopped walnuts
Whipped cream

Place Melba sauce in bottom of parfait glass, combine ice creams and add to glass, sprinkle with walnuts, garnish with whipped cream.

Coupe Valencia

1 scoop vanilla ice cream
1 scoop orange ice
2 tablespoons chocolate sauce

Whipped cream
Maraschino cherry

Combine ice cream and ice and place in parfait glass, cover with chocolate sauce, garnish with whipped cream and cherry.

Coupe Argentina

1 scoop vanilla ice cream
1/2 scoop pistachio ice cream
1/2 scoop raspberry ice
2 tablespoons Melba sauce
  (bottled)

Whipped cream
1/2 slice canned pineapple
Maraschino cherry

Place ice cream and ice in parfait glass, cover with Melba sauce, garnish with whipped cream and top with pineapple and cherry.

Coupe Java

1/2 banana (sliced)
1 scoop coffee ice cream
1 scoop vanilla ice cream

2 tablespoons caramel sauce
Whipped cream

Place sliced bananas in bottom of shallow serving dish. Combine ice creams and add to dish. Cover with caramel sauce, garnish with whipped cream.

Coupe Cecilson

1 scoop strawberry ice cream
1 scoop chocolate ice cream
2 tablespoons chocolate sauce

5 black cherries (pitted)
Whipped cream

Place ice cream in parfait glass, cover with chocolate sauce, garnish with cherries and whipped cream.

Coupe Chartreuse

1/2 apricot (canned)
1 scoop vanilla ice cream
1 scoop strawberry ice cream
1 jigger Chartreuse liqueur

1 tablespoon Melba sauce
 (bottled)
Whipped cream

Place apricot in bottom of shallow serving dish, combine ice creams and add to dish. Top with liqueur and Melba sauce, garnish with whipped cream.

Coupe Palm Beach

1 scoop orange ice
1 scoop lemon ice
2 orange sections

1/2 slice pineapple (canned)
Whipped cream
Maraschino cherry

Place ices in parfait glass, garnish with orange sections, pineapple and whipped cream. Top with cherry.

Coupe Riviera

4 candied marrons (chopped)
1 scoop vanilla ice cream
1 scoop chocolate ice cream
2 tablespoons Melba sauce

1 tablespoon mixed fruit, chopped
(canned or fresh)
Whipped cream

Place marrons in bottom of parfait glass, add ice creams, cover with Melba sauce, garnish with chopped fruit and whipped cream.

Rainbow Parfait

1 scoop strawberry ice cream
1 scoop vanilla ice cream
1 scoop pistachio ice cream

2 tablespoons crushed
strawberries

Pile the three ice creams in a parfait glass, top with crushed strawberries.

Nesselrode Parfait

*2 tablespoons nesselrode sauce
(bottled)*

2 scoops rum raisin ice cream

Combine in a parfait glass.

Neapolitan Parfait

*1 scoop strawberry ice cream
1 scoop pistachio ice cream*

1 scoop vanilla ice cream

Combine in a parfait glass.

Parfait Apricotine

*2 tablespoons apricot jam
2 scoops vanilla ice cream*

Whipped cream

Melt jam over low heat until just liquid, pour into bottom of parfait glass, cover with ice cream, garnish with whipped cream.

Parfait Mont Blanc

*1 scoop pistachio ice cream
1/2 scoop peach ice cream*

*1/2 scoop lemon ice
Whipped cream*

Combine ice creams and ice in parfait glass, garnish with whipped cream.

Petits Fours

1/4 pound almond paste (may be purchased in gourmet food shops)
1 cup sugar
8 eggs
1 cup butter
1 teaspoon vanilla

3 cups cake flour
3 teaspoons baking powder
Fondant icing (see below)
Almond slivers or maraschino cherries
Walnut halves or candied fruits

Combine the almond paste with ½ cup of the sugar, add 1 egg and blend well.

Cream the butter with the remaining sugar. Add the remaining eggs, one at a time, beating well after each addition. Stir in the vanilla, then the almond-sugar mixture and beat until smooth.

Sift the flour with the baking powder and add it, about ½ cupful at a time, to the batter, beating well after each addition.

Spread the batter in a well greased 10- by 16-inch sheet pan (or two square cake pans) and bake in a preheated 350°F. oven until firm and lightly browned (about 30 minutes).

Cool cake in pan. Cut into small squares or diamonds. Ice each with fondant icing (below) and decorate with candied cherries, fruits or nuts.

MAKES: about 4 dozen petits fours.

FONDANT ICING

3 cups sugar
1 1/2 cups water
Flavoring

1/8 teaspoon cream of tartar
Food coloring

Combine the sugar and water in a saucepan, place over medium heat and stir constantly until sugar is dissolved. Add the cream of tartar and cook, without stirring, to soft-ball stage (240°F. on a candy thermometer), wiping the sugar crystals which form on the inside of the pan with a pastry brush dipped in water. Remove from heat and pour into 2 or 3 separate bowls. Add a different flavoring and a drop or two of food coloring to each. Place the bowls in a large pan of hot water. Spear the cut cake squares or diamonds with a fork and dip them, one by one, into the fondant. Place when dipped on a cake rack to cool. (If the fondant becomes too thick before all the cakes are iced, thin it with a small amount of boiling water and replace the water in the pan holding the bowls of fondant with fresh boiling water.)

Madeleines

The recipe for madeleines remained a secret for a very long time. It is said that it was sold for a very large sum to the pastry makers of Commercy who made of this great delicacy one of the finest gastronomic specialties of their town.

MADELEINE DE COMMERCY

1 1/4 cups superfine sugar
2 1/4 cups sifted cake flour
3/4 teaspoon soda
Pinch of salt

7 large or 8 small eggs
Grated rind of one lemon
1/2 cup plus 2 tablespoons melted
    clarified sweet butter

Sift sugar with flour, soda, and salt into large mixing bowl. Add eggs and beat to a smooth batter. Fold in lemon rind, then slowly add melted butter, beating constantly. Beat batter with a wire whisk until light and creamy.

Butter and lightly flour small shell-shaped madeleine molds or fluted tartlet molds and fill ⅔ full of batter. Bake the madeleines in a preheated 400°F. oven for 25 minutes.

MAKES: about 3 dozen small madeleines.

PLAIN MADELEINES

1 cup superfine sugar
2 cups sifted cake flour
Pinch of salt
6 eggs

1 cup melted and clarified butter
1/2 teaspoon vanilla or almond
    extract

Sift sugar, flour and salt into large mixing bowl. Add eggs and beat to a smooth batter. Slowly add melted butter, beating constantly. Add flavoring and beat batter until light and creamy.

Butter and lightly flour small shell-shaped madeleine molds or fluted tartlet molds, and fill ¾ full of batter.

Bake the madeleines in a preheated 400°F. oven for 25 minutes.

MAKES: about 2 dozen madeleines.

Marrons aux Kirsch

1 19-ounce jar marrons glacés   2 tablespoons butter
   (imported glazed chestnuts)   1/3 cup Kirschwasser
Ice cream

Drain syrup from chestnuts and place in a chafing dish with butter. Cook, stirring very gently, over low flame until heated thoroughly. Adjust heat to high and pour in the Kirsch. Let it boil up, then tilt the pan toward the flame so that the fire "jumps into the pan" and ignites the Kirsch. Allow to flame briefly. Spoon flaming over ice cream or, if preferred, over sliced fresh strawberries.

Orange Sabayon

6 egg yolks   1/2 cup fresh orange juice
3/4 cup sugar   1 teaspoon grated orange rind
1/2 cup white wine   1 tablespoon orange liqueur

Beat egg yolks in top of double boiler with wire whisk until light and "lemony." Beat in sugar and place over barely simmering water. Add wine, orange juice, rind and liqueur. Continue to beat until mixture begins to thicken. Pour into sherbet glasses and serve warm.

SERVES: 6.

Peach Tart

Pastry dough for 9-inch pie shell
Raspberry jam
3 or 4 thin slices of sponge cake
8-10 peach halves (canned) and
    juice

1/2 cup currant jelly
Sweetened whipped cream

Line a 9-inch pie plate with pastry dough, pressing it against the bottom of the plate. Prick the bottom, line it with aluminum foil and fill with dried beans. Place in a preheated 350°F. oven for 10 minutes. Remove the beans and foil and bake until golden brown, about 5 minutes.

Cool, then cover the pastry with a thin layer of jam. Cover jam completely with thin slices of cake, trimmed to fit the pan. Pour peach juice over cake, cover cake completely with peach halves, cut side down.

Heat the jelly in top half of double boiler over hot water. When liquid, pour over surface of peaches. Refrigerate tart until well chilled.

Slice and serve each portion garnished with sweetened whipped cream.

SERVES: 8.

Strawberry Mousse

1 cup milk
6 tablespoons sugar
3 egg yolks, lightly beaten
1 teaspoon cornstarch
1 envelope of unflavored gelatin,
    softened in 2 tablespoons cold
    water

1 cup heavy cream
3 egg whites
1/2 cup fresh strawberries,
    crushed
Whipped cream
Whole strawberries

Scald the milk with 2 tablespoons of the sugar in a large saucepan. Remove from heat.

Combine the egg yolks with the cornstarch and a second 2 table-spoons of the sugar. Beat with wire whisk until well blended, then slowly add to the hot milk, stirring them into the milk with a whisk as they are added.

Place mixture over medium heat and cook stirring with a wooden spoon until thick. Remove from heat and stir in softened gelatin. Set aside until cool.

Beat the cream until stiff. Beat the egg whites in the second bowl until stiff and fold in the remaining sugar.

Fold the beaten cream, the egg whites and the crushed strawberries alternately into the cooled custard.

Pour mixture into 8 lightly greased individual molds or one 2- to 2½-quart mold, and refrigerate until firm.

To serve: Dip molds briefly into hot water and unmold onto serving plates. Garnish with whipped cream and whole strawberries.

SERVES: 8.

Bombe Vesuvius

1 quart raspberry ice	*Candied violets*
1 quart vanilla ice cream	*Warm water*
Egg shell	*Dry ice*
Whipped cream	

Let raspberry ice and ice cream stand at room temperature until slightly soft. Do not, however, allow to melt.

Spoon raspberry ice into a well chilled 2-quart mold. Using the back of a large spoon, draw the sherbet up the sides of the mold and press to form an even layer on bottom and sides, leaving the center hollow.

Fill center with vanilla ice cream. Cover mold with foil, seal by pressing foil against sides of mold and place in freezer until ice and ice cream are very firm.

Dip mold briefly in hot water, invert onto a chilled platter and unmold. With a teaspoon, scoop out a small hollow in the center of the ice cream and place the egg shell in this indentation. Surround shell with a border of whipped cream and decorate bombe and cream with candied violets. Just before serving, fill egg shell half full of warm water. Add a small piece of dry ice and bring bombe to the table smoking with a volcanic effect.

SERVES: 6.

NOTE: Individual bombe molds may be made instead of a large mold. Proceed in the same manner.

Profiteroles au Chocolat

1 *cup milk*
4 *tablespoons butter at room*
  temperature
1 1/2 *cups flour*
1/2 *teaspoon salt*

2 *teaspoons sugar*
3 *large or 4 small eggs*
Chocolate ice cream
Chocolate sauce
Whipped cream

Place milk and butter in a large saucepan over medium heat and bring to boil. Add the flour all at once and stir rapidly until mixture forms a stiff dough and leaves the sides of the pan. Remove from heat, add salt, sugar and 1 egg; beat until smooth. Add remaining eggs one at a time, beating well after each addition.

Place rounded teaspoonfuls of batter on an ungreased baking sheet about 2 inches apart. Bake in a preheated 400°F. oven for 10 minutes. Reduce heat to 325°F. and bake a final 20 to 25 minutes. Do not open oven door first 25 minutes of baking.

Cool puffs on cake rack.

When ready to serve, cut a slit in one side of each puff and fill with chocolate ice cream.

Place 3 or 4 filled puffs in each dessert dish. Cover with chocolate sauce and garnish with whipped cream.

Peaches Armagnac

6 *large ripe but firm peaches*
Boiling water
3/4 *cup sugar*
1 1/2 *cups water*
1/2 *cup Armagnac (substitute Co-*
gnac or other brandy, if desired)

12 *thin slices of sponge cake cut in*
circles, or sweet biscuit rounds
1 *cup crushed sweet macaroons*

Plunge peaches in boiling water. Rinse under cold water and slip off skins. Cut in half and remove seeds.

Combine sugar and water in large saucepan, bring to boil. Lower heat, add peaches and Armagnac. Simmer gently until peaches are tender. Cool in syrup.

To serve: place peach halves, cut side down, on rounds of sponge cake or sweet biscuits. Spoon a little of the syrup over the surface and sprinkle with macaroon crumbs.

SERVES: 12.

Strawberry Shortcake

2 *cups fresh strawberries, sliced*
4 *tablespoons sugar*
6 *dessert biscuits (see below)*

4 *tablespoons Kirsch*
1 *cup heavy cream*

Place strawberries in a nonmetal bowl, add 2 tablespoons of the sugar and 2 tablespoons of the Kirsch. Refrigerate covered one hour or longer.

Whip the cream until stiff, whip in remaining sugar and Kirsch.

Spoon strawberries over warm biscuit halves. Cover with whipped cream.

DESSERT BISCUITS

2 cups flour, sifted	3 tablespoons vegetable
2 teaspoons baking powder	shortening
1/2 teaspoon salt	1 tablespoon butter
1 tablespoon sugar	3/4 cup milk

Sift flour, baking powder, salt and sugar into large mixing bowl. Cut in shortening and butter until mixture resembles coarse-ground cornmeal. Add milk all at once and mix to a smooth dough. Turn out on a lightly floured board and knead lightly. Roll out to ½ inch thick and cut with biscuit cutter. Place on ungreased baking sheet and bake in a preheated 450°F. oven for 12 to 15 minutes.

MAKES: 12 large or 24 small biscuits.

Baba Miguette

1/2 cup milk	1/4 teaspoon salt
1 envelope active dry yeast	1/2 teaspoon lemon rind
2 cups flour	1/2 cup butter, melted and cooled
2 whole eggs	3/4 cup water
2 egg yolks	1 teaspoon lemon juice
1 1/2 teaspoons sugar plus 1/2 cup sugar	1/4 cup rum

Scald the milk, pour it into a large mixing bowl and cool to lukewarm. Add the yeast and set aside until dissolved. Stir in ¾ cup of the flour and mix to a smooth dough. Cover bowl and set aside in a warm place until double in bulk.

Beat the whole eggs with the yolks in a second mixing bowl. Add the 1½ teaspoons sugar, the salt, lemon rind and cooled melted butter. Stir in the remaining flour, blend well. Combine with yeast dough and blend until smooth.

Butter individual baba molds and fill half full with dough. Cover molds and set aside in a warm place until dough rises to the rim of the molds.

Bake in a preheated 350°F. oven until babas are firm and lightly browned. Remove from molds and cool on cake rack while preparing rum syrup.

Combine the ½ cup sugar and the water in a saucepan. Place over moderate heat and allow to simmer gently for 10 minutes. Remove from heat, add lemon juice and rum.

Place babas in a shallow nonmetal pan and pour the hot syrup over them. Turn them several times in the syrup and let cool.

Serve each baba with a scoop of ice cream. Garnish with sweetened whipped cream.

MAKES: 12 small babas.

Waldorf Frozen Cake

1 quart praline ice cream
1 9-inch sponge cake (homemade
or bought from a good bakery)
1 pint heavy cream

1/4 cup sugar
Walnut halves
Candied fruit

Spread soft ice cream in two 9-inch layer-cake pans. Cover pans with foil and place in freezer until ice cream is very firm.

Cut cake into three thin layers.

Dip ice cream-filled pan briefly in hot water and unmold onto bottom layer of cake. Cover with second layer of cake and repeat with second layer of ice cream. Top with third layer of cake.

Press cake and ice cream together and place in freezer while whipping cream. Whip cream until stiff, fold in sugar. Spread on frozen cake, covering it completely. Return iced cake to freezer until cream is very firm.

Decorate surface of cake with walnut halves and candied fruit.

SERVES: 8.

Soufflé Citron

1/2 cup finely chopped candied citron
2 tablespoons Kirsch
4 tablespoons butter at room temperature
4 tablespoons flour

2 tablespoons sugar, plus 1/3 cup sugar
1 1/2 cups milk
5 egg yolks, well beaten
4 egg whites

Place citron in nonmetal bowl and add Kirsch. Set aside 30 minutes or longer.

Cream the 2 tablespoons butter with the flour and sugar until smooth. Beat until light and fluffy.

Place milk in large saucepan, bring almost to a boil. Add the creamed butter mixture and stir rapidly until smooth. Remove from heat, cool slightly, then stir in the beaten yolks. Beat the egg whites in a separate bowl until stiff. Beat in the ⅓ cup sugar and fold this meringue into the soufflé batter. Blend quickly but well and pour at once into a 2-quart well-buttered soufflé dish. Place immediately in a preheated 375°F. oven and bake for 30 minutes or until soufflé is well puffed and lightly browned.

Serve at once with apricot sauce.

SERVES: 4 to 6.

Oscar's Chocolate Marble Cake

1 cup butter at room temperature
1 3/4 cups sugar
3 cups flour
1/4 teaspoon salt
1 tablespoon baking powder
6 eggs, lightly beaten
1 cup milk

1/2 teaspoon vanilla
1/2 teaspoon lemon extract
4 squares unsweetened chocolate, grated
Chocolate fondant icing (see below)

Cream the butter with the sugar until light and fluffy. Sift the flour with the salt and baking powder.

Combine the eggs and milk and blend with a wire whisk. Add the dry ingredients alternately with the milk-egg mixture to the butter and sugar, beating well after each addition. Mix in flavoring.

Put ⅓ of the dough in another bowl, add the grated chocolate and blend well.

Spoon alternate layers of white and dark dough into a well-greased 9-inch tube pan. Place in a preheated 350°F. oven and bake 45 to 50 minutes or until a cake tester (or toothpick) inserted in the center comes out clean.

When done, remove cake from oven and let stand 10 minutes. Loosen sides and invert on cake rack for 5 minutes. Remove cake from pan and allow to cool before covering with icing.

CHOCOLATE FONDANT ICING

3 tablespoons butter	*2 squares unsweetened chocolate,*
1 cup confectioners' sugar	*melted*
1/2 teaspoon vanilla	*Milk as needed*

Cream butter with sugar, stir in vanilla and melted chocolate and blend until smooth. Add sufficient milk to make a smooth but stiff icing.

Lemon Sponge Pudding

2 cups milk	*3 tablespoons water*
3 egg yolks, lightly beaten	*1 envelope unflavored gelatin*
1/2 cup sugar	*1/4 cup lemon juice*
1 tablespoon cornstarch	
2 egg whites	*1 cup heavy cream*
1/3 cup sugar	

Scald the milk. Cool slightly. Mix egg yolks with sugar and cornstarch in top half of double boiler. Place over hot but not boiling water. Add the scalded milk, beating constantly. Cook, stirring frequently, until custard thickens and coats the spoon.

Sprinkle water over gelatin to soften and stir into warm custard. Cool custard to room temperature. Stir in lemon juice.

Beat egg whites until frothy, then slowly beat in sugar a little at a time, beating after each addition. Continue beating to a stiff and shiny meringue.

Beat cream until stiff. Fold first meringue, then cream into custard. Pour into molds rinsed with cold water. Refrigerate until firm.

SERVES: 8 to 10.

Fried Ice Cream

1 pint pistachio ice cream (substitute other flavor if desired)	Grand Marnier liqueur, about 2 tablespoons
3 tablespoons all-purpose flour 1 egg yolk 1 whole egg	1/4 teaspoon salt 1/2 teaspoon sugar 1 cup milk
Egg wash—of one egg beaten with one tablespoon water 1–1 1/2 cups grated coconut	(substitute crumbled macaroons or vanilla wafers if desired) Bland vegetable oil for frying

Using a tablespoon, form 8 balls of ice cream about 2½ inches in diameter. Dip your hands in ice water and smooth them as evenly as possible. Make a small hole about ¼ inch deep in the center of each ball.

Place them not touching on a flat tray or a double thickness of aluminum foil. Place in freezer and freeze until very firm.

Combine flour, egg yolk, whole egg, salt and sugar. Blend until smooth. Add milk, beat well and strain through a fine sieve. Set batter aside 1 hour before making crepes.

Heat a 5- to 6-inch crepe pan. Grease lightly with butter. Pour in about 2 tablespoons of batter. Quickly rotate pan so batter spreads over bottom evenly. Cook over medium heat until underside is lightly browned and top is firm. Turn and cook second side until brown flecks appear.

Continue until all batter has been used. Cool crepes thoroughly before proceeding.

Remove ice-cream balls from freezer and fill hole ¾ full of Grand Marnier liqueur. Cover top of hole with a little soft ice cream, smooth over and return balls to freezer until again frozen solid.

Rub edges of each cooled crepe with egg wash. Place frozen ice cream ball in center. Fold crepe around ice cream enclosing it completely. Roll filled crepe first in egg wash, then in coconut. Return as soon as prepared to freezer. Freeze one hour or longer.

Fill deep heavy skillet to about 3 inches of rim with bland vegetable oil. Heat to 350°F. on deep fat thermometer (or until small cube of soft white bread will brown in 35 seconds). Remove ice cream-filled crepes from freezer and plunge into the hot fat for 20 seconds. Remove immediately and serve at once.

MAKES: 8 fried ice-cream balls.

NOTE: Batter makes about 16 5-inch crepes. Stack leftover crepes with wax paper between each, wrap stack in foil and refrigerate or freeze. Use in any recipe calling for crepes or sprinkle with confectioners' sugar, dot with butter, roll up and bake in a 350°F. oven until well heated.

Serve with morning coffee.

Chocolate Cream Pudding

1 4-ounce bar semisweet
   chocolate, grated
2 cups milk
1/4 cup sugar

4 egg yolks
3 whole eggs
1 teaspoon vanilla

Melt chocolate in top half of double boiler over simmering water. Combine with milk and sugar.

Beat the egg yolks with the whole eggs until light and lemon colored. Add the chocolate-milk mixture, beating constantly. Add vanilla, strain through a fine sieve and pour into small earthenware pots or custard cups.

Set the pots in a pan of water. Cover pan and bake in a preheated 350°F. oven for 15 minutes or until custard is firm. Refrigerate until well chilled. Serve with whipped cream.

SERVES: 6.

Hilton Orange

8 *large thick-skinned oranges*	4 *egg yolks*
1/2 *cup sugar*	3/4 *cup heavy cream*
1/3 *cup water*	
2 *egg whites*	1/4 *teaspoon cream of tartar*
2 *tablespoons sugar*	

Cut a thick slice from the top of each orange, scoop out juice, fruit, pulp and seeds (reserve fruit and juice for another use). Trim a little of the skin from the bottom of each orange shell so that they will stand steadily upright. Be careful, however, not to cut through the skin.

Dissolve the sugar in the water in a saucepan. Bring to boil, lower heat and simmer gently for five minutes. Cool.

Beat egg yolks with wire whisk in top half double boiler until light and lemon colored. Add the cooled syrup in a slow, steady stream, beating constantly. Cook stirring over hot (not boiling) water until custard becomes creamy and thick. Remove from heat and cool to room temperature.

Beat the cream until stiff. Fold in the cooled custard. Pour mixture into orange shells. Arrange them not touching in a shallow pan. Freeze until firm.

Beat egg whites with cream of tartar until frothy. Beat sugar in gradually, a little at a time. Continue beating to a smooth and glossy meringue.

Top each frozen orange shell with meringue. Place in a preheated 400°F. oven until lightly browned. Serve at once.

SERVES: 8.

Lukshen Fruit Kugel

1/2 pound noodles	1/2 cup chopped raisins
2 eggs, separated	1/2 cup peeled and chopped
2 tablespoons chicken fat (or	apples
vegetable oil)	1/4 cup broken nut meats
2 tablespoons sugar	1/4 teaspoon cinnamon
1/2 teaspoon salt	1/8 teaspoon nutmeg

Cook noodles in boiling salted water until tender. Drain but not too dry; moist noodles make a more tender pudding. Beat egg yolks with fat, sugar and salt. Combine with noodles. Fold in the fruit, nut meats and spices. Beat egg whites until stiff and fold into noodle mixture. Pour into a well-greased casserole and bake in a preheated 350°F. oven for 45 minutes or until surface is nicely browned.

SERVES: 6.

Sherry Trifle

3 eggs, slightly beaten	1 9-inch sponge-cake layer
1/2 cup sugar	2 tablespoons strawberry jam
1 teaspoon cornstarch	1/4 cup chopped toasted almonds
2 cups milk	1/4 cup crumbled macaroons
1 tablespoon butter	Sweetened whipped cream
1/2 cup sherry	Whole toasted almonds

Combine eggs, sugar and cornstarch in top half of double boiler. Beat with wire whisk until smooth. Scald milk in separate pan, add slowly to egg mixture, beating constantly. Cook, stirring, over hot water until custard thickens and coats the spoon. Remove from heat. Add butter and ¼ cup of the sherry. Stir until butter is melted and blends into custard. Cool.

Cut sponge-cake layer lengthwise into two thin layers. Spread with jam, put back together and cut into 1-inch cubes.

Spoon a little of the custard in the bottom of 8 custard cups. Cover with cake cubes. Sprinkle cake with remaining sherry, add chopped almonds and crumbled macaroons. Cover with custard to the top of the dish. Refrigerate covered 3 to 4 hours (or longer).

To serve: Unmold onto flat dessert plates, garnish with sweetened whipped cream and whole almonds.

SERVES: 8.

Grasshopper Parfait

1 cup boiling water
1 package lime-flavored gelatin
1/2 cup cold water
2 tablespoons crème de cacao

3/4 cup green crème de menthe liqueur
1 cup heavy cream

Pour boiling water over gelatin. Stir until dissolved. Add cold water and ½ cup of the crème de menthe. Blend and pour into shallow pan. Refrigerate until firm.

Whip cream until stiff; fold in remaining crème de menthe and the crème de cacao.

Place chilled firm gelatin in a cold mixing bowl. Using two table knives, cut into very fine dice.

To serve: Place alternate layers of the diced gelatin and the whipped cream in parfait glasses, ending with cream.

SERVES: 6 to 8.

Noodle Pudding

1 pound flat noodles
2 eggs, separated
4 tablespoons chicken fat or
  vegetable fat

4 tablespoons sugar
1 teaspoon salt
1/2 cup raisins

Cook noodles in boiling salted water until tender. Drain but not too dry; moist noodles make a more tender pudding. Beat the egg yolks with the fat, sugar and salt. Mix with the hot noodles. Beat egg whites until stiff but not dry and fold into noodle mixture. Fold in raisins. Pour into a greased 8½-inch square pan. Bake in a moderate oven (350°F.) for about 30 minutes. Raise heat slightly last few minutes of baking to brown top.

SERVES: 10.

Baked Grapefruit

1 large grapefruit
2 tablespoons Cognac or
  fine brandy

2 tablespoons honey
1 tablespoon brown sugar

Cut grapefruit in half. Remove seeds with sharp pointed knife. Separate pulp from pith all around grapefruit. Loosen pulp from dividing membrane. Sprinkle each half with one tablespoon Cognac, one tablespoon honey and ½ tablespoon brown sugar. Place in a baking dish containing about ¼ inch water. Bake in a preheated 400°F. oven for 15 to 20 minutes. Serve hot.

Excellent for Sunday breakfast or for a late supper snack.

SERVES: 2.

Western Spice Cake

1/2 cup butter or margarine	1 teaspoon cinnamon
1 1/2 cups dark brown sugar	1 teaspoon nutmeg
3 large eggs	1 teaspoon allspice
2 cups sifted all-purpose flour	1 teaspoon vinegar
1 teaspoon baking powder	1 cup milk
1 teaspoon baking soda	1 cup chopped prunes
1 teaspoon salt	1 cup chopped walnuts

Cream butter or margarine and brown sugar; add eggs, one at a time, beating after each addition. Sift together flour, baking powder, baking soda, salt, cinnamon, nutmeg and allspice. Add vinegar to milk. Add flour mixture and milk alternately to creamed mixture, mixing well after each addition. Add prunes and walnuts to batter. Pour into 9-inch greased tube pan. Bake in moderate oven, 350°F., for 1 hour, or until done. Cool 5 minutes in pan. Remove and cool on wire rack. Frost, if desired, when thoroughly cool.

GENERAL INDEX

RECIPE INDEX

NOTES